"This deftly written collection satisfies one of our deepest curiosities: 'What's it like being her? Or him?' Paul Zimmer's answer takes us there by way of steam engines, gray foxes, dray horses, Big Joe Turner, a French dentist *trés sympathique*, tumbledown shacks, Duke Ellington's riffing to empty seats, and a fellow poet heroically obscure, except in Zimmer's moving homage. To know ourselves we people-watch life-long, yet glean only vague suppositions. In contrast, these quietly impressive sketches—so much bigger than their pages—add up to a self-portrait humane and intimate as kinship."—Reg Saner

"This is a delicious assortment of essays. They are witty and poignant and convey an astonishing range. My favorite is 'Mon Dentiste' in which the author in his mangled French names himself a retarded poet, but every reader will find something special here."—Maxine Kumin

"This is an inspired, inspiring book, as honest as the broad, fertile fields of the American middle west. Paul Zimmer, long known as an important poet and editor, gives us a story told in essays of recollection that are connected—as those fields finally are—by the diminishing sound of our railroads. In prose as clean-limbed and supple as a boy who climbs a tree, Mr. Zimmer writes of war, poetry, domestic happiness, a life lived with books, and the need to examine one's past—as well as the nations'—with real feeling but with no sentimentality. This is a wonderful achievement."—Frederick Busch

"Paul Zimmer's *Trains in the Distance* is a captivating blend of memoir, philosophy, and plain good story-telling (with some astonishing stories told). It gives us a large helping of the poet Zimmer has always been, with a taste of Ben Franklin and a touch of Mark Twain."
—Madison Smartt Bell

Trains in the Distance

Trains in the Distance

Paul Zimmer

The Kent State University Press · Kent and London

May 2005
From Wisconsin, for Al
+ Grace, with gratitude
for you kind words about
my writing and thanks
for your continuing friendship
and care.

love,
Paul

© 2004 by Paul Zimmer

All rights reserved

Library of Congress Catalog Card Number 2003021740

ISBN 0-87338-796-1

Manufactured in the United States of America

08   07   06   05   04   5   4   3   2   1

Library of Congress Cataloging-in-Publication Data

Zimmer, Paul.

Trains in the distance / Paul Zimmer.

p.   cm.

ISBN 0-87338-796-1

1. Zimmer, Paul—Homes and haunts—Ohio.

2. Poets, American—20th century—Biography.

3. Zimmer, Paul—Childhood and youth.

4. Ohio—Social life and customs.

5. Ohio—Poetry.

I. Title

PS3576.147Z476 2004

811'.54—dc22

2003021740

British Library Cataloging-in-Publication data are available.

To Suzanne 〜

When in disgrace with Fortune and men's eyes
I all alone beweep my outcast state,
And trouble deaf heaven with my bootless cries,
And look upon myself and curse my fate,
Wishing me like to one more rich in hope,
Featur'd like him, like him with friends possess'd,
Desiring this man's art, and that man's scope,
With what I most enjoy contented least;
Yet in these thoughts myself almost despising,
Haply I think on thee, and then my state
(Like to the lark at break of day arising
From sullen earth), sings hymns at heaven's gate,
For thy sweet love rememb'red such wealth brings,
That then I scorn to change my state with kings.
　　　—William Shakespeare, Sonnet 29

Contents

Acknowledgments ❧

This book describes incidents and experiences in the author's life and reflects his opinions regarding these events. Some names and identifying details of individuals mentioned in the book have been changed to protect their privacy.

The author and publisher are grateful to the following publications for permission to reprint the following essays in this book. "Big Joe Turner" and "My Afternoon with Duke" were originally published in *Brilliant Corners*. "Real Words" and "William Metts, American Poet" first appeared in *New Letters*. "The Commissioner of Paper Football" and "Small Places" originally appeared in *Shenandoah*. "The Gray Fox" was first published in *The Gettysburg Review*. "The Trains" first appeared in *The Georgia Review* and subsequently in *September 11, 2001: American Writers Respond*, edited by William Heyen (Silver Springs, Md.: Etruscan Press, 2002). "Mon Dentiste" appeared in *The Connecticut Review*, in a slightly altered form. "The Grass" and "The Mechanics" were first published in *The Great River Review*.

I wish I could personally thank everyone who has helped me with this work. Jim McKean, Brendan Galvin, Erik Zimmer, Bill Ford, and Gary Gildner endured some of the early drafts, but many other great friends and readers provided stories, sustenance, encouragement, and warmth. I do not trust my memory to make the list complete, but like all writers, I am dependent on the generosity of others.

Part One ~

Where is the boy
Who looks after the sheep?
He's under a haycock
Fast asleep.
   —*Little Boy Blue*

The Trains

Our house in Ohio was near a railroad spur, and freights rumbled nightly through my flawless sleep into my dreams. In daylight my friends and I played near the tracks and waved to trainmen as the locomotives chuffed past our neighborhood like big dogs breathing hard.

But steam engines were headed toward extinction after World War II; the great machines were being supplanted and torn apart for scrap-metal. It gave me a helpless feeling to witness their passing, like watching old ballparks or venerable buildings being demolished. It was a hard transition, and things have never been quite the same. But I still pause to watch and listen to the forlorn honking of their ugly children, as the diesels slink under the interstates and skirt the edges of our towns, and I still do a lot of railroad dreaming.

Trains pass through most of the writings in this book at some point, carrying manifest and passengers, rumbling through the middle of narratives and stitching things together, or perhaps just thrumming and hooting distantly as they round the far curve of a story.

There have been no trains where I live now in southwestern Wisconsin for more than sixty years; the final run on the fifty-two mile track of the bankrupt Kickapoo Valley and Northern branch line, running from La Farge to Soldiers Grove, passed through in 1939. I guess it was a sad occasion and the local bands played funeral dirges as the engine paused at each station.

All of the old KV&N track was pulled up for scrap-metal during the war and only a few old stations and traces of the throughway are left. Ben Logan, the novelist who grew up in this area, tells me that on damp days the sound of those old trains winding through the valleys and woods came right up to your ears and made you feel the sadness of the fog. For a few moments it took you away from whatever you were doing.

I would give a great deal now to hear that mournful hooting in the woods, the old clinkers spouting soot and cinders into the trees and onto the board-and-batten houses near the tracks. It would give more of a frame to this landscape than the remote wisps and distant droning of high-flying jetliners over our ridge.

But I start this piece on September 12, 2001, and today I long to hear the distant drone of the high liners and see their contrails criss-crossing overhead. The skies are empty and we are in national shock, mourning death and devastation as we begin to gain determination. We are in a state of war, and we are told that it might be extended and cruel. In a few weeks or months, when we have gathered our wits and resources, we will be mounting our response, sending young men and women off to distant battlefields. They will say goodbye to the people they love. It will be the fifth war of my generation's time.

Why do I sit at my writing table at a time like this? Because it is what I know how to do. Perhaps I should admit that I long for another time, sights and sounds I never knew or deserved to know—steam trains in the valley below, slogging through the rain, or rolling buoyantly in sunlight. I want to hear the creak of solemn engines and boxcars as they twist through misty woods and fields in the valley below.

My orders in 1955 were to report to the army's base near the atomic test grounds in Nevada. I was not going to war, but I was headed toward the unknown and particular danger of my era. I had been ordered to participate with a small group of men as a military participant in the testing of these ultimate weapons. I did not know what this meant, but I was aware of what the bombs had done to Hiroshima and Nagasaki a decade before. The army wanted to test the reactions of soldiers to atomic explosions, and we were to witness detonations at very close range.

What I saw and experienced in Nevada does not matter at this moment. What I want to remember here is what I felt—or what little I felt—as I rode the train west from Ohio. I was twenty years old and this was my first train journey alone. I had taken a few days' leave from the army to visit home on my way to Nevada. I said hello and good-bye to my friends. My mother tearfully held me for a long time at our house, but she did not go to the railroad station. My father, who never cried, took me to the train and resolutely shook my hand as I stepped up into the coach. He tried to say something, but the engineer was clearing blast pipes on the big engine, so we shook our heads, smiled, and waved at each other through the din. Then my father turned and walked away quickly with his head down.

I was a shy, taciturn young person and had learned in basic training to attract as little attention as possible to myself. Frightened and trying to be brave, I was also numb with uncertainty. The trip took several days, and I must have changed trains in Salt Lake City. We passed through grand vistas, deserts and mountains I had never experienced, but I paid little attention. I nibbled candy bars and ate the sandwiches my mother had packed in a shoebox. Without speaking, I pointed to my selections of soft drinks from the vender's cart. Mostly I kept my head down, reading and talking to no one.

What was I thinking? I cannot recall. I was doing my duty, traveling toward danger, preparing myself to be staunch. I had a book, an anthology of great short stories, and I had some vague notion that I wanted to be a writer. This was my first experience of Chekhov, Saki, Huxley, Conrad, Maupassant, Colette, Mann, Turgenev, Welty, Salinger, Porter, Hemingway, Faulkner. Frequently I was puzzled by what I read, but when I finished the book, I started it again.

There was a young woman with a baby in the seat across the aisle. The baby was colicky, and the mother struggled to comfort it. At one point, in frustration, she appealed generally to the passengers, asking if someone could help her open a can of baby food. She had forgotten a can opener. I carried an army C-ration opener on my key chain. When no one else came forth, I motioned to her that I could give assistance. She smiled with relief and thanked me when I handed the opened can back to her. She told me that her husband was also in the army; she wanted to have a friendly chat, but I did not know how to respond. I blushed and put my nose back into my book of stories. I must have opened half a dozen cans for her during the trip, working the sharp little blade around their rims, then handing them back without a word.

When I made my way to the restroom at the end of the car, I kept my eyes straight ahead and looked at no one. How can I explain my extreme reticence? I was so lonely and unpracticed, so far from home. I did not know how to speak, nor did I have anything to say. Occasionally I gazed out the window, but mostly I read.

I recall pondering and rereading Joseph Conrad's story, "Youth," the old man's narrative of his perilous experience as a young seaman on a storm-wracked, burning coal liner. I wondered what he meant when he said toward the end: "I remember my youth and the feeling that will never come back any more—the feeling that I could last forever, outlast the sea, the earth, and all men; the deceitful feeling that lures us on to joys, to perils, to love, to vain effort—to death."

I think about myself as that disoriented young man on the train, as I think of the young people who will soon be loading their gear, saying good-byes, and heading toward the highly ambiguous future with so little knowledge of the past. I think of what they must do in the days and months and years ahead, their silence, their fear and determination. I stand in a meadow and look up, wishing for vapor trails in the crisp, autumn sky. I listen longingly for the clatter of old trains in the valley below.

Rose Court

Miss Hanna was the fury of Rose Court, the alley that ran behind the houses on our block. When we played catch on the gravel she lurked in her boxwood shrubs. If we missed a throw and the ball rolled onto her property, she charged out to snatch it like some mad virago.

"You should be ashamed!" she shrilled as we skedaddled. "I'm going to call the welfare man."

It was 1940, I was six years old, and war talk made everyone jittery, but I had never seen anyone act like Miss Hanna. My friends and I ran from her as if she were the devil's sister. Mother would find us panting and whispering on our back porch. When we told her what had happened she grew reflective.

"She didn't threaten to hurt you or grab at you, did she?"

"No, but she screamed at us!"

"You must try to understand. Miss Hanna's not right. She's alone all the time. It affects the way she acts."

"But she took my ball."

"I'll get you another," Mother said. "Think of it this way. What if you had no one to care for you and only yourself to talk to. It would make you sad and sometimes you would find things to be angry about."

But I was a little boy and did not share mother's empathy for lonely, eccentric women. My father had no such forbearance. After supper we would go out to Rose Court for some catch. One evening as we played, I saw Miss Hanna come out from her house and pretend to work in her flower garden. I knew from experience that she was lurking. One of my errant tosses rolled across her line. She ran to snatch it, then charged out, blanched and hideous in her fury, onto Rose Court.

My father, at first startled by Miss Hanna's tantrum, soon returned her fire. He was a considerate man and tried to tell Miss Hanna that her claims were unreasonable, but his tone grew louder as she maintained her shrill assault. I was impressed and proud of his bravery in the face of what had always seemed to me the gravest danger. Miss Hanna began to back away.

"Give back the baseball!" Father demanded. Miss Hanna dropped it as she retreated, howling over her shoulder that she was going to report us to the welfare man.

Dad and I resumed our catch, but his heart was no longer in it. When we went into the kitchen he asked my mother, "Who is the welfare man?"

"Miss Hanna's been at it again, hasn't she?"

"She's had a job keeping records in the freight shed at the Pennsy station for twenty years. Mickey Belinski says she knows how to keep the stuff rolling, and they take good care of her. She just had her house painted. She can't be on welfare. What is she talking about?"

"Some fantasy of hers, I guess. The welfare man is someone who will protect her. If that's the worst she can threaten us with, she's quite harmless."

"She steals my baseballs!" I reminded them, but no one acknowledged this.

"I feel sorry for her," Mother said at last.

"She can't act like that and expect pity." Dad angrily stirred sugar into his cup of coffee and flattened out the evening paper. "I don't care if she does have some loose screws."

A few days later I was practicing with my bat in our yard and accidentally tapped a ball over the fence onto Miss Hanna's lawn. I did not think she was home, but even the slim chance of one of her fanatical blitzes made my scalp freeze.

I looked over the fence at my baseball nestled in her grass and considered all the dangerous possibilities. Finally, I pulled myself up over the weathered four-by-fours and wire fencing and dropped down onto her grass. When I hit enemy turf my heart was walloping the inside of my ribs. It was perhaps my first act of true courage.

Miss Hanna had been watching. She charged howling from her back door, her glasses askew and flashing, words strident and incomprehensible. I was ambushed in the middle of enemy territory, and did not know how to stand and fight against such ferocity. The blood fell back from my skin and I feared for my life. Terror drove my retreat and as I scrambled back over the boards I gashed my arms and legs on Miss Hanna's rose bushes. I lay wounded in our yard as her caterwauling face loomed over the fence above me.

I was up and barreling toward the safety of our house, when the screen door banged and Mother emerged. She was transformed; her fuse lit at last, her anger incandescent. I had never seen her in such a state.

"Give him back his ball," Mother said with restraint that belied her anger.

"I'm going to call the welfare man," Miss Hanna said.

"Call the welfare man, call the police, fire department, the mayor while you're at it," my mother exploded. "I'm tired of being nice to you. You are an old fool. We are the only people in the neighborhood who speak to you. No more! Give him back his ball."

Miss Hanna was unraveled, daunted at last. She turned to walk away with the baseball still in her hand.

"Give the ball back!"

Miss Hanna turned and tossed the ball back into our yard. When we went back into the house, Mother was crying with anger. She paced the kitchen and slammed a pan down on the counter. She did not curse, but her words burned in her wake. When she saw that I was bleeding, her tears and anger increased as she bathed my wounds and dabbed them with Mercurochrome.

I was sorry to have caused such trouble—but then again, not so sorry. I was glad for what seemed to be resolution, and somehow it made me feel important to have caused such serious rumbling amongst the adults. I was glad to have been defended by my mother. It gave me a feeling of security. I felt revenged, yet I worried that that she was so upset.

None of us ever spoke to Miss Hanna again. She stopped lurking in the bushes and a few weeks later she put out a "For Sale" sign. Mother was pensive and saddened when she saw this, but Dad told her not to feel guilty.

I observed them all carefully—Mother, Father, and Miss Hanna—and did not know what to feel, except that I was glad to be able to play now without fear. When the moving truck came for Miss Hanna's things, I could not escape a sense of guilt for having been involved in these events. But the feeling did not last long and I went on with my life.

This is a small story. Most people have similar tales to tell. The details—Miss Hanna's gray, angry face and her strange territoriality; my outright fear; my mother's determined attempts at tolerance, her compassion, her attempt to entreat, then her full scale fury; my father's exasperation and firmness, the words that were spoken in anger—have stayed with me all my life. They settled into my consciousness, becoming emblems for certain basic human feelings. In these voices responding to Miss Hanna I heard the whole world of response that I would one day need to remember, and come to understand.

Here are some of the words I used to tell this story: *fury, shame, charge, enemy, violation, retreat, threaten, protect, blood, fanatic, ambush, fear, bravery, charge, dead, courage, terror, explode, curse, rage, tears, scourge, wounds, trouble, resolution, combat, facedown, security, guilt, revenge.* Made into a list, they seem more abrasive than when they appear tucked into the text of this story of childhood. They are the same words I heard used to describe World War II. They are words that became temporarily quiescent in our vocabulary a few years later when we were at peace.

But once again they are part of the atmosphere; they are the words our leaders use daily in their speeches and briefings. The news networks and press spray them in all directions like herbicide. They are present in our psyches, even when our computers and televisions are dark.

The language is ancient. Four centuries ago, in Act 4 of *Henry V*, as the battle of Agincourt approaches and through its course, Shakespeare puts the following words into the mouths of his characters. They are some of the same words that appear in my Rose Court story: *danger, courage, pain, dead, enemy, fear, vengeance, assault, death, guilty, fight, perilous, angry, blood, wounds, kill, brave, gash, burn, rage.*

I randomly open a copy of Winston Churchill's *Blood, Sweat, and Tears* and read from page 213 through 215. Here are a few words the anguished but resolute prime minister used in his prose sixty years ago: *ferocious, threats, malice, cruelty, wanton, destroy, murder, break, suffer, grievous, loss, bad, attack, broken, menace, grisly, loss, retribution, spite, fear, aggression, fierce, mournful, death, brutish, burn, rage.*

These are words we use to define our condition when we are threatened. They describe our feelings, tell us what we must face, and describe our resolution. On Rose Court or in grim times they are inescapable. In our anger and anxiety, the words of compassion and civility are suppressed in our consciousness. Perhaps there is no antidote in times of peril, but there is danger that the omnipresence of these violent words in our talk over a long period might permanently affect our ethos, that we might forget who we are, or should be, beyond defending ourselves.

I knew a hog farmer from Missouri when I was in the army. He once described to me how the slaughtering was done on his farm; how he and his brothers would chase the pigs down and drag them to the father, who held a knife at the slaughter board. The father cut each animal's throat and the boys strung it up on a rope by its hind legs to bleed. After slaughtering a number of pigs, the father would call a halt to the work and make them go for a cool drink from the well, and then to sit in the shade of the barn for a spell. He warned of a condition called "bloodlock." He claimed that if you let this work possess you, you might go on killing forever.

Here is a small list of words, taken at random from the writings of Henry David Thoreau: *nature, goodness, genius, holy, life, compassion, faith, friend, happiness, respect, sensitivity, wildness, silence, seasons.* I offer them as a drink of water, a cool respite in the barn. As our sensibilities are assaulted in times of threat, as language heightens, words such as these, if we have the discipline to remember them, can continue to signal the presence of hope, the redemptive power of the natural world, great art, and humanistic thought. We forget them at our peril.

Monument Hill

We sledded down 14th Street hill and heard a morning train barging through the drifts. I was out early with Frank Callison and Randy Bogart after an all-night snowfall. By the time we reached the slope above the tracks we saw the locomotive below us, working hard and making more noise than usual. It was one of the big, downgraded ten-wheel steamers that pulled through our neighborhood three times a day and twice in the middle of the night with loads of coke and iron bars.

As we stood looking down at the big engine, Randy dared Frank, "Let's go down and look close." He was always challenging Frank to do stupid things. It was his way of covering up being scared of Frank. I stayed out of it. They dropped belly first onto their sleds and I grew anxious as I watched them streaking down through the windswept powder on the hill. Bogart turned his sled and flopped off halfway down, but Callison kept barreling toward the big blue train as it erupted violent smoke through curtains of flying snow. The engineer hit his brake and shrilled his whistle. I could see the circle of bolts on the smoke box and the cowcatcher spraying out white as the connecting rods locked wheels on the buried rails. Empty coal cars banged and wavered behind.

Callison disappeared in white scud; I heard his sled crunch under the massive wheels and fell to my knees on the road. Bogart rolled over on the hillside below me, opened his mouth and stared up at the hell-bent, gray clouds.

The train wobbled on down the line, metal shrieking on frozen metal. Finally, with an enormous bang, the engineer got it stopped. I was sobbing and Bogart wailed at the sky. I put my forehead down in the snow and rocked back and forth. The locomotive hacked in the distance.

Wind folded the loose snow and there was an acrid smell in the air. I heard trainmen shouting, jumping out and running back along the track.

My parents had given me a globe for my birthday and I spent hours studying it. Canton was not shown, but I imagined that our neighborhood was a tiny speck in northeastern Ohio on the rounded world. If you could drill a hole directly through the earth from our neighborhood you might come out in western Australia.

I rode my bicycle around with a clipboard and mapped the houses and streets of our small patch of the earth. My family's frame house on McGregor Avenue sat in the middle, two blocks below Taggart's Ice Cream Store and four streets above where the earth curved down to the railroad tracks beside the park.

Frank Callison lived two blocks away in the direction of Monument Park. I won't say that he and I were close friends, but we walked to school together most days and avoided Bogart. Frank liked to come by my place early so he could plunk on our upright piano in the living room while I finished breakfast. His family had been broken by divorce, and he seemed to enjoy the way things fitted together in our house. We shared interest in baseball and catching frogs, and both of us had stamp collections.

Unlike Bogart, Frank had no need to talk all the time. His level of boyhood combat and sports achievement spoke for itself and was on a much higher plain than ours. I was grateful that he would stick up for me when I was in a scrape. Frank had little to prove; we admired and surrounded him, and he walked in our midst. I don't know why he allowed himself to be baited or why he went ripping down that slope toward the train.

Randy Bogart was the son of a high school principal. I could not understand why he was such a compulsive craphead. He was boorish, relentless, and stuck to you like a swatted fly. He knew I couldn't stand him and seemed to enjoy this. If I tried to avoid him, he'd chase me down and sit on me until I said uncle. When he wasn't pushing me around, he enjoyed shocking me in the basest terms with his explanations of the facts of life and death. He was the first person to describe sex to me.

"Don't you *know?*" he was incredulous. He loved to show me up. Other boys surrounded us and I was on the spot. "The man puts his prick into a woman's pussy and passes seeds into her."

Seeds. I thought about seeds, the scratchy carrot and radish seeds I helped my mother plant. Then I thought about my poor little penis. I had never seen a vagina. "Doesn't it spill?" I asked, a remark that set the others rolling in the grass.

Bogart was not as sanguine on the subject of death, but his explanation of the end was more imaginative. "Everything stops," he said. "Your eyes don't see and you are done. Your blood freezes and you don't breathe. Only your soul goes on. It rises up like a bird through the sky to heaven. If you've been bad it falls down a volcano to hell in the center of the earth, and you scream and burn forever."

We lived in a town where death was memorialized. President William McKinley had been born near Canton, and his monument stood on a hilltop near where we lived in town. My dad reminisced about when it was being erected in the early part of the century. He was just a kid, but he remembered steam shovels and loads of huge, trimmed stones that rolled in on the trains. "They built it like a beehive," he said. The marble dome loomed over our neighborhood. If I stood on a chair and stretched high, I could see it from the top corner of our attic window. Not every kid in America could claim such a thing. It gave me a sense of pride and place to live just blocks from the tomb of an assassinated president. There were reminders of McKinley's death and sacrifice everywhere—memorial plaques and streets named after him. The postcards on the drugstore racks showed solemn views of the monument and surroundings.

Sunday mornings after mass, Dad and I sometimes walked through the park, up the hill, and into the cold mausoleum to gaze at the black, elevated sarcophagi containing McKinley and his wife. McKinley had been shot a long time ago, but there were still dusty wreaths and purple mourning ribbons on steel stands below the entombed bodies. The big dome was built for sadness, the light was dim, and our footsteps resounded when we moved about. Death was the business here, and it was even more serious than a bank or church.

∾

The stopped locomotive chuffed in the distance. In my anguish, down on my knees, I saw something move through the steam and smoke that hung beside the tracks. It came up the hill, wavering like a ghost.

Frank Callison, his face whiter than the flurries, his stocking cap down over one eye, made his way up through snow-tufted weeds toward us. Bogart made a sound like air running out of a punctured tire. We rose to our feet and ran to touch Frank. Somehow he had rolled off his sled just before it went under the wheels. We could see the trainmen coming now, three of them loping through the snow along the tracks toward us.

"Let's get out of here!" Bogart said, and we bolted, bounding back up through the snow on 14th Street hill, our sleds wobbling on their ropes behind us. It was the only thing we could think to do. Bogart tried laughing as we ran, but Frank and I did not take it up.

I felt strangely fugitive, suddenly emptied. I wasn't cold anymore. When we reached the top of the hill we paused to catch our breaths. I could see the monument looming through the falling snow, on its rise above our neighborhood. Even if you turned away from it, it was always just over your shoulder.

None of us thought about the anguished trainmen finding pieces of Frank's sled, scrambling under the cars and searching through the brush for his body. We decided not to go home and ended up in Bogart's garage, stomping around trying to stay warm. Randy and I chattered with relief, making a pact never to tell anyone what had happened, but Callison did not join in our gabble. He sat slumped on a stack of old tires with his hands jammed into his mackinaw pockets. He had pushed his stocking cap back and there was an ugly bruise on his forehead.

"You okay?" I asked him.

"Yeah," he said, lifting his chin slightly. He was still Frank Callison, blond and muscular, the best of us all. Now he had survived. As always we deferred to him, even in his silence.

Although we did not discuss it, we all felt guilty, knowing we had caused great trouble and concern. We expected the arrival of authorities at any moment.

Randy and I made up a nervous game, running like Indians and firing darts at a patchy deer head hung on a garage stud. When I broke one of the deer's glass eyes, Bogart gave me a shove. "That's it!" he announced. "I'm freezing my ass off. The train's probably moved on. We can go down to 12th Street and cut over to monument hill."

The snow on the slope was too deep for good sledding, but we did not want to go home yet. We stood at the top of the hill, clapping our mittens together for warmth. Finally Frank, without saying anything, took Randy's sled, pushed and wriggled through the heavy white, laboriously working his way down the long, long slope to the bottom to make a track for us. We stood at the top and watched with admiration. "That bugger has strong legs," Bogart admitted.

We spent several hours exhausting ourselves, joylessly plunging down the hillside, then dragging the sleds back up toward McKinley's huge tomb. Callison remained distant and silent. He took turns riding piggyback with us. After one of his runs down with me we stood together brushing off snow. Frank suggested, "Let's ditch Bogart. Come on, let's walk around to the other side and see if the snow plows are coming through."

"Fuck you guys!" Bogart shouted at us from the top of the hill as we struggled through the drifts away from him, around the foot of the slope to the parking area and the long, wide, marble stairs leading up to the dome. Part way up on a landing the bronze statue of William McKinley was mounted. From below we could see snow piled on his green brow and shoulders.

"He looks like Santa Claus up there," Frank said. "Let's go have a look." We trudged up the deeply drifted steps and stood together gazing at our slain president, shot by a crazy man, his silhouette cold and eminent against the overcast, his square head crowned with white.

There was a sudden break in the clouds and brightness made my eyes ache. Some blue jays fussed around the statue and one of them landed on the president's head, dislodging a sparkle of snow onto his shoulder. The sky closed up again; it grew darker and the flurries resumed. Frank stooped to make a snowball and threw it at the blue jay. He wiped his nose with his wet mitten and I saw the muscles in his cheeks flex.

The blue jay flew to a shrub along the rail, shrieking and gargling at us. Frank bent over to scoop up more snow, but the bird had flown off by the time he stood up. Frank had a way of looking serious. He'd purse his lips and turn his head to the side.

"My stepdad knows a lot," he said. "He's always telling me stuff. He told me McKinley lived a week before he died, and he still had bullets in him."

The Commissioner of Paper Football

I ∾

> The dusky wolf bays,
> Shaft meets shield. The moon meanders
> Behind glowing clouds; wicked acts
> Will provoke fierce battle.
> Awaken, my warriors!
> Take up shields and gird yourselves,
> Stand and be brave again!
> —*The Battle of Maldon*, A.D. 991

In 1946 some of the Cleveland Brown football players kept themselves in condition during the winter by playing exhibition basketball against pickup teams in northern Ohio. The Knights of Columbus Hall had a gymnasium and the Browns came to Canton one February night to play a team of ex–high school stars.

My uncle was an executive for one of the sponsoring steel mills, so my cousin and I had first row seats. When the Browns arrived, strapping in their big overcoats, making no eye contact with anyone, as is the way with the huge and famous, they sauntered through the crowd to their dressing room. We were awestruck and cheered them prodigiously.

One of the Browns' managers spotted my Uncle Walt and brought Marion Motley, the great fullback, over to introduce him. Motley was one of only a handful of blacks playing professional football in those days. As he amiably pumped my uncle's hand, I got a close-up view of his brawn. He noticed me gaping and turned to envelop my twiggy white fingers in his great hand.

"What's your name?" His smile was imposing and complete.

"Paul. . . ."

"You gonna be a football player, Paul?" he asked as he gently shook my hand.

"Yes, oh, yes, yes, yes."

Some nights when I cannot sleep I lull myself by slowly reciting the names and evoking the images of my 1946 Paper Football League All Star team. I have done this for more than half a century. I envision them one after another in their poses; the linemen down in their crouches: center, Frank Sniadack of Columbia over the ball; guards, Walt Vezmer of Michigan State and Jim Lecture of Northwestern; tackles, Jim Coppinger of Arizona and Arnie Weinmeister of Washington; ends, Hubert Bechtol of Texas and Bob Ravensburg of Indiana; the backs dashing and leaping: quarterback, Ernie Case of UCLA; halfbacks Charlie Trippi of Georgia and Fingerface Ted Tannehill of Southern California; fullback, Vic Schwall of Northwestern.

If I am still awake when I get to the end of the lineup, I go on to recall some backup players; usually centers, because I was the pivot for the St. John's Grade School Crusaders in 1946 when we were runners-up in the Parochial League. I have always been proud of the centrality of my position, believing it is the beginning of things, the convergence of stirring developments. I say Bob Orlando of Colgate, Joltin' John Cannady of Indiana, Bill Walsh of Notre Dame, or Jim Enos of Army. Usually by then I start to drift sweetly off.

These were the All Stars of my Paper Football League and I was commissioner, head of all franchises, and chief manipulator of the momentous action that occurred in that dynamic organization in the mid to late 1940s. There were four teams made up of players whose pictures I had cut from *Street and Smith's Football Pictorial Yearbook, 1946*. The league schedules were long, extending into the winter months. There was glory in those games and disappointment, too. The play was an imitation of life, and I made it all up myself.

In my hometown football was emphatic ritual. The spirit of the game dwelled in the sooty, autumnal air of the place. Some of the first professional football games were played in Canton. Jim Thorpe, Pudge

Heffelfinger, and other legends had roamed our gridiron. Johnny Blood probably missed his first bed check in my hometown. Even before the Pro Football Hall of Fame was installed in one of the parks, football was a staple of the environment.

In nearby Massillon, nurses placed toy footballs in the cribs of newborn male infants. Little boys and big boys put on pads and helmets. As the poet James Wright wrote, in towns like Canton, young boys "grow suicidally beautiful / At the beginning of October, / And gallop terribly against each other's bodies."

2 ⟨⟩

In 1946 there were eight million people dislocated in Europe, the first meeting of the General Assembly of the United Nations was held in London, American labor unions were striking extensively after the lifting of government wartime restrictions, the Nuremberg Trials were progressing, Winston Churchill declared that an "iron curtain" had come down across Europe, and the United States exploded two atomic bombs off Bikini Atoll.

1946 was the year of the fabled Army–Notre Dame game, the epic of my childhood. The Black Knights of the Hudson versus the Fighting Irish. West Point trains officers for military service, so during the war years it retained great athletes to play football; but teams from schools like Notre Dame were stripped by the military draft. It seemed almost patriotic for the Army and Navy teams to pound out lopsided victories, while Notre Dame especially paid dearly, losing to Army by brutal scores like 48 to 0 in 1945. It was hard for Catholic boys.

But in 1946 The Fighting Irish were stocked with tough returning war veterans like Emil Sitko, Johnny Lujack, and George Connor, and by November, as both teams remained unbeaten, the day of reckoning was approaching. The excitement and build up in the newspapers and on the radio captivated us for weeks, as war news had held us rapt just a few years before.

Because my parents worked in retail stores on Saturdays, on game day I had the house to myself. I spread my green bed cover over the stainless steel kitchen table and marked out yard lines with string. I had green marbles for Notre Dame, black marbles for the Cadets, and I taped the player's names to the marbles with bits of adhesive tape. I tuned in the big Philco in the living room, and as Bill Stern gave his histrionic account of the action, I moved the players up and down the field, waiting for the explosion of points. Stern could make a two-yard gain sound like a blitzkrieg, so I remained expectant.

But by the fourth quarter there was still no score. Noted for their powerful offenses, it was generally forgotten that those sixty-minute players also excelled on defense. Their coaches, Red Blaik and Frank Leahy, were cautious strategists and risked little, so the game was put-and-take. Eventually I stopped moving the marbles up and down the field and went to lie on the couch to listen. The game ended in an exasperating scoreless tie and the Catholics were not revenged in 1946.

In my hometown in the mid-to-late forties it did not matter if you were brilliant or beautiful in school—if you did not have a letter on your sweater you were second-class. You cowered to the side in the hallways with sissies, debaters, thespians, valedictorians, fudge packers, choir singers, and other nondescripts, while the bozos plunged down the middle, whacking each other on the biceps and strolling with the prettiest girls.

Going out for football was the first official test of manhood. If you did not at least try to make the squad, you had to wonder what this signified for the rest of your life.

My father had a curvature of the spine and had not been able to play football. This was a problem for me when other boys bragged about their fathers' heroics. Once, to my everlasting shame, when I was angry with him, I castigated him about this. But my father did not pretend about it. My uncles and many of the neighborhood men claimed that they had played football. Most of them, I eventually discovered, had not—or if they had, they were cannon fodder on practice squads. But they felt it was important to make this claim, even if they had to hedge a bit. Their attitudes and the central metaphor of their male talk ranged around football: "cut him down," "try an end run," "hunker down," "fake him out," "reverse fields," "out of his league," "hit the line," "go for blood."

I could perceive no acceptable alternatives to football, and this created difficulty for me. I was not cut out for glory and the pads. As I write this, even after all the years, I still feel a residue of inadequacy. I missed something that I was not capable of having, something that belonged only to the strongest. It's an old story, like the mad regret or guilt some men feel because they have not fought in a war.

My football career lasted one year. I had been pushed around enough by my grade school mates to realize that I did not have the ability to stand out on the gridiron. But in my class there were twenty boys, and a few of them were even less capable than I of participating in football. In the eighth grade I banged and heaved as best I could at practice, and hung around until I was named starting center for the St. John's Grade School Crusader football team. Father Lattau, our coach, observed that I was at least able to get the ball back to the quarterback before I was knocked flat—so I performed a necessary function. I weighed eighty-five pounds and had my clock cleaned regularly.

St. John's playground was covered with gravel and slag from the mills; it was no place to practice football, so we used a level open field in Stadium Park, just down the hill and across the railroad spur from my house. One late afternoon I was walking down 12th Street to practice when Father Lattau picked me up in his black Plymouth coupe. A freight train was running through on the tracks and as we waited at the crossroads Father observed, "A football team is like a railroad train."

I thought about this for a while. Gary Beadle was our tough, star halfback, so I said, "Yes, and there's the engine out there in front running like Gary."

Father Lattau didn't take this up right away. It was a long train. Finally, he said, "No, Zimmer. That's you out in front. The center. Nothing goes without you."

There were enough good athletes on the Crusader team that we eventually got to the championship game, played in front of an early crowd before Central Catholic High School's Saturday afternoon game with Youngstown Ursuline.

My teammates and I felt gloomy about our chances. St. Joseph had beaten us badly in the regular season, and we had little hope. Gary Beadle wanted to try to buck us up. He asked Father Lattau for permission to address the team privately before the game, claiming he had something to say that might give us motivation. When we gathered around Gary, anxious for his inspiration, he said that his neighbor lady had bet her entire paycheck on us. If we did not win she would go hungry. We had to triumph for her.

Well, it wasn't exactly a Knute Rockne exhortation, but for some reason Gary's message stirred me. By God, there was no reason for a St. John woman to have to go hungry! I went onto the field and crashed my skinny frame furiously into St. Joseph's players large and small. I was the center. Nothing was going to go without me. I was fearless and motivated. For fifteen minutes I was Frank Sniadack of Columbia or Joltin' John Cannady of Indiana. The St. Joseph's players had not counted on me as a force, so I surprised them and sent them sprawling play after play as I raged around the field.

At the height of my frenzy, I lost control and punched their middle guard, Emil Fazio, a significant specimen, who had mugged me badly in the previous game, and was ejected from the game. I complained to the referee that I had only been retaliating, but he waved me off the field. The St. John's crowd cheered me as I took my time trotting to the sideline and slammed my leather helmet down in front of the astounded Father Lattau.

We lost by a close score and I regretted socking Fazio, believing we might have triumphed if I had not been so impulsive. I had become a force, a tiger ripping holes for our running backs, a frenzied eighty-five-pound rhinoceros leveling all things in my path. At long last I was feeling the spirit of football—my moment of glory—but it was too late.

I had talked so much football at home, bragged so roundly on my performance in the grade school championship game, that I was compelled to try out for the high school team. I still weighed under a hundred pounds, but there were no excuses. The coach of the freshman team was Dale Fuller, a former fullback for a small Ohio college team, a swaggering stallion in white socks, high-topped cleats, tight T-shirt, and football pants. It seemed as if he had been born to wear such things. He wore a whistle on a chain around his neck and his haircut made his head look like an artichoke. He did not want any one-hundred-pound centers on his squad. He had already spotted his athletes. His method for eliminating the rest of us scrawny doormats was to humiliate us until we disappeared. His most potent technique was to line us up for tackling practice against the varsity backs and let them shred us. He especially enjoyed putting me up against the starting fullback, Buddy Bolender, who would bring his knees up hard into my face and bloody my nose as I clutched futilely at his pumping legs.

Bruised and humiliated, after some days I announced at home that I was terminating my effort to make the team. My mother especially was disappointed. She had been a cheerleader in high school. "We were looking forward to going to games and rooting for you," she told me.

3 ∾

My feeling of inadequacy endured for a long time. There was no substitute for football, no way to soften my disillusionment. But at least I was a good dreamer. I had created my Paper Football League when I was in grade school and now in my early high school years I took it up again in earnest. When you are a dreamer, if you cannot satisfy others, you must satisfy yourself. I was captain of my fantasy, the Commissioner of Paper Football.

The Street and Smith Football Yearbook had cost me a quarter in 1946 when I bought it off the rack in Hoobler's Drugstore. I took it in my hands, gazing at the photographs and reading the team descriptions as if they were scripture. The pictures dazzled me, beginning with the color cover of the barbarous-looking USC tackle, John Ferraro, in his crouch. Inside were black and white photographs of players, mostly with their helmets off, dashing, hunkering down, making flying tackles, plunging, leaping to throw or catch passes, all of them dedicated and deadly serious, the backs looking fleet and canny; the linemen scowling as if they were preparing to eat babies.

Among three hundred posed photographs of players from across the country, there is only one black included, a full-page image of John Reagan of Montana, his legs spread, football cocked to heave downfield. In the team description it says Reagan is from Chicago, a war veteran, "the first negro to be commissioned by the Navy." All of the hundreds of other players in the Yearbook look menacing, scowling and deadly serious. Only Reagan, amongst these, is smiling engagingly as he looks downfield, preparing to throw the ball.

In the yearbook there were action shots as brutal and awe-inspiring as scenes painted by Delacroix or Goya, with captions that read, "Skladany (40) Pitt end with Ralno puts crusher on Zaboric, of Illinois." The posed pictures included the famous and redoubtable Doc Blanchard and Glenn Davis of Army, John Lujack of Notre Dame, Choo Choo Justice of North Carolina, and Bobby Layne of Texas; and then there were the less famous players, whose pictures I carefully cut from the magazine and arranged to form the four teams of my paper football league.

The schedule was long, extending into the winter months. I timed the games on my alarm clock—each lasted half an hour—and played kneeling on a pillow at my bedside, manipulating the action on top of the green bedcover. At first my play was violent; I held the pictures in my hands and dashed them together. Every tackle was a gang tackle. If a player was torn, it was an injury and he had to be attended. If it was a partial rip, he could be repaired with scotch tape and go on playing. But if he was ripped in half, he was out of the game.

It was a primitive contest, requiring a maximum of fanciful, boyish invention. I loved my league and played it endlessly, keeping careful records of passing and touchdowns. We did not have computer games or virtual reality in 1946, but we had imagination.

Fingerface Ted Tannehill was my star runner and best athlete. I clipped his picture from an action photo; a tackler had grabbed Tannehill from behind with his hands over his face. The caption read, "Something new in tackles as Bob Nelson, WU, stops Tannehill, USC." I cut out Tannehill's photo with Nelson's fingers over his face. Somehow this seemed appropriate—Dick Tracy was a prominent comic strip in those days, and Fingerface could have been one of his grotesque enemies. Fingerface became the fastest and most elusive runner in my league. I even cheated for him on occasion, zipping him along to make his runs more spectacular.

Ernie Case was my most adept passer. He is depicted leaping into the air heaving a left-handed jump pass, a pose favored by sports photographers of those days. My players assumed personalities and quirks. Case was mercurial. Fingerface was proud. Vic Schwall, my most devastating power runner, was truculent and difficult to control, and his line plunges were greatly feared. I even mounted his picture on cardboard to make him more durable. When he hit the line, guards and tackles were sometimes cleaved in two. Wounded players were borne off the field on top of a Tootsie-Toy ambulance.

I used John Reagan of Montana only as a substitute in my league. I think I was puzzled and overpowered by him as I had been by Marion Motley. I felt somehow that I did not know how or did not have the right to use him often. I remember feeling strange about this paper racism.

By early winter, as my league continued its long schedule, it became evident that some of the more active players were in such bad condition they would not be able to complete the season. I needed to purchase another copy of the Yearbook and cut out replacement pictures—but of course there were no copies available of a two-year-old football annual.

I decided to write to Street and Smith; but in my youthful uncertainty, felt they might be suspicious of someone ordering a football annual in February two years after publication. I also worried that they might suspect I was cutting their publication to shreds with my scissors. I was not going to admit that I had already purchased a copy. My letter was apologetic and I lied a little. I don't remember the exact message, but it was something like this, scrawled in my wobbly, Palmer Method longhand:

Dear Sir,
I was sick in 1946 when the College Football Yearbook came out. I am putting in a quarter and hope you will send me a copy. Sorry I missed it. I really like your magazine.
Sincerely,
Paul Zimmer

I taped a quarter to the letter. Two weeks later a copy of the Yearbook arrived, rolled up and put through a #10 envelope sealed and split at both ends.

I stopped buying football annuals many decades ago, but this past autumn, out of curiosity I bought *Street and Smith's College Football Yearbook* off a stand in the super market. It cost me seven bucks and is computer designed like *People* or *Vogue*. There are fancy statistics, highlights, ratings, prognostications, and team accounts, all written in zippy talk like a printed television sports cast. The individual pictures of players are all action color shots labeled only with their names. They grimace anonymously behind their face-guards, and display little personality. There are no wondrous picture captions, as in 1946: "Big Cheek, Okla. Aggies giant tackle, measures Utah back, Warner, and that was that." Or "Clyde Scott is Navy's best fullback if he is right. But coaches are worried. He had a bad foot at spring drill." Or "Bill Hart, guard for A&M, was captured 3 times by Germans."

There are 120 players pictured in the current edition, eighty of them are men of color. There is an image of an intense young black man, Yohance Humphery, a Montana running back dashing past a fallen tackler. In the team account it says he is "the school's all time leading rusher." I wondered fleetingly if he had broken John Reagan's record.

As a cynical experiment—more than half a century after I had written my original February letter—again I wrote to Street and Smith in my even more uncertain longhand. I wrote in winter, sending the same message as in 1946. I included seven dollars folded and scotch-taped to the letter. There has been no response.

I still remember when a quarter was worth something, but this year a friend, scanning the Internet, found listed on eBay for fifty dollars a copy of the *Street and Smith Football Pictorial Yearbook, 1946*. I did not hesitate. My hand trembled as I wrote the check, ordering my third copy of the yearbook—fifty-five years after its publication. I cannot describe my excitement when it arrived by priority mail. I opened the package, reading slowly and savoring the yellowed pages; then again even more deliberately, permitting the glorious memories to roll.

There they were still, heroic and dashing—De Moss of Purdue soaring to throw a jump pass, McLellan of Brown diving savagely like a huge hawk through the air at the camera, Reader of Michigan State, Moncrief of Texas, Fritz of Maryland, Huffman of Tennessee, Castleberry of Georgia Tech, Biles of Army, Luongo of Penn, Ficklin of Utah. And there was John Reagan of Montana, he alone smiling, his strong legs spread as he prepared to fling a football downfield.

Yeomen all, every one of these talismans of my pubescent years. I did not dwell long on how all these men, if still living, are now approaching eighty-years old. I am sixty-eight myself, my knees grind, my scissors are dull, my imagination centers on other things. But still, on some long nights, I evoke those husky phantoms.

The crows turned scarlet from warrior's blood.
The army charged with their chieftain.
For a year I'll sing songs of their triumph.
When I'm ancient and declining to death,
I'll not be content unless praising them.
—*The Battle of Argoed Ilwyfain*
Taliesen, Welsh, Sixth Century

An Unsentimental Education

In the long nights of aging I have a few recurring bad dreams. One of the very worst is that I am drafted into the army again. I tearfully bid good-bye to my family and go off to basic training. I cannot persuade the officers that I am almost seventy years old. I am compelled to march endlessly, fire guns, throw grenades, and crawl muddy infiltration courses. Exhaustion consumes me, I grow near to death, but the drill continues.

But even more upsetting are my education nightmares. Grade school, high school, college. In all these school dreams I am in misery again. Puzzled and bored by class work, I abandon all hope of doing well and fear the imminent crash that will occur when grades are issued at the end of the term. These school dreams are based on a reality that I suppressed for years as I made my living and lived my life.

I was a uniformly lousy student. It was not a familial problem—my parents and sister had been good at school. All my friends were excellent students. I was alone in my disgrace. Occasionally I managed to rally a bit, but I had no good years in school. I pretended that it did not matter to me. It was a hard way to grow up, requiring self-delusion and fakery, a constant scramble to find reasons for believing in myself. But as the nuns always told me—I had no one to blame but myself.

Why would I want to ponder these youthful failings at this late stage in my life? Does it matter now? The bad school dreams reoccur, not as often as before, but often enough, and I awaken feeling stupid and inadequate. I wonder, have I always been an artful dodger, masking my shortcomings? Or has my whole life been a reaction to these early failures? Do I feel cheated? Was it my own fault?

I remember thinking it was cool to say that school stinks. Where did this attitude come from? Why do I write about these difficulties? Who really cares? I do. It is for me to remember. Perhaps I seek expiation, some kind of atonement that will make the dreams go away. By digging and reflecting a bit I might intercept some of the darting pains that rise yet from old scars. Generally I have repressed my school experiences or pretended that they now amuse me. But they were no joke. Those years were a cruel sentence when I was enduring them. I never felt even hopeful of doing well.

Is it possible that subconsciously I only wanted to be a writer, even at that early age? Was I unwittingly creating my own curriculum?

I could not memorize well. I was bored by windbags. My attention span was friable. I could not diagram a sentence. But I could write, I could create, I could imagine with words. No credit was given for this. Was I simply not meant for school? Was something psychologically or physically wrong? I carry the stigma yet and anything that resembles a formal test daunts me. If I am having my eyes or ears tested and think I am missing things, I grow anxious.

I was in second grade. Sister Marie Nativa said, "house." I squirmed in my desk, thought as hard as I could, and didn't have a clue. I printed, "rquyt" on my tablet. Sister Marie Nativa said, "grass." I wasted less time thinking this time, and scribbled, "xrnfovi." Maybe I would get lucky and hit one right. Maybe she wouldn't look at my paper. In any event, I did not care. My Lord! I *really* did not care. I just wanted to get on with things, wanted school to disappear. Everyone else around me cared and worked to do their best. But no shame, threat, punishment, scolding, ruler rapping, nor extended grounding could make me really care. I do not know why. I felt helpless, swore to everyone that I was doing my best, but neither the nuns nor my family believed me.

My mother and father were loving and nurturing, but they were frustrated. I was their disgrace. The nuns sent my papers home with notes: "I don't know why Paul is doing poorly. He is intelligent. Can you urge him to pay attention?"

My parents and I would begin our discussions calmly, but I was already on the defensive. What else could I do? I tried to claim to my parents that the nuns did not like me or that I was threatened and distracted by bullies on the playground. I recall once my parents asked me if I could see well. I was a desperate kid. I could see perfectly, but I told them that words looked wavery on the blackboard and even drew a sample for them—

dog.

They didn't believe me. My mother asked me to try harder. My father ordered me to try harder. School was important. They wanted to be proud of me. I must pay attention. I would be sorry if I didn't.

Well, I was already sorry, but I could not bring myself to bear down. Perhaps it was attention span deficiency or some form of dyslexia. Was it laziness? Was I just a stupid kid? It went on and on—through high school and then college. I was marginal, not infrequently less than marginal, but I was able to concentrate on things that interested me. I liked words. I followed baseball assiduously and kept detailed records. I created elaborate games and sports leagues. I listened carefully to music, read Classic Comics, organized tidy collections of boyish things, and built marvelous hideaways. It is not an impressive list, but it meant something—and I was not a total clod. At the very least, I was giving off some interesting signals.

There is another partial explanation—perhaps the real root of my problems. Because I was born in mid-September, I had just turned six when I was enrolled in the first grade. I had not been sent to nursery school or kindergarten. Most of my mates were at least six months older than I was. That is an important time when one is growing up. I was out of my league in grade school from the start, and this perhaps set a pattern, was a psychological gap that I never really overcame.

St. John's Grade School drew students from all ends of town. Some children came to school in dirty hand-me-down clothes. The popular ones wore bright sweaters and new corduroy. I was an in-between baby in that classroom, physically, economically, and intellectually, and because I was not a snappy student, I fell in with rowdy kids on the playground. But I was not tough either and had to rely on skillful bluffing. It didn't last. I had little credibility and paid up not only in the classroom, but also on the playground cinders. Often I just walked around by myself, pretending to be occupied and happy. I liked to go home and play in my room for hours, or run around with my non-Catholic friends in the neighborhood, who were not as much sorted out by toughness or smartness.

My sister was in the seventh grade at St. John's when I was in the first. She was exemplary in every way, but I did not know how to follow her example. One day, I bumped into an older boy on the playground and we started punching and kicking. My pants were torn and my shirt was stained with slag grime and blood from my nose. The nun was appalled and sent for my sister to come to our classroom. The scene became a protracted nightmare, unraveling out of control in front of my class. The nun told Beverly that, not only was I doing poorly in my class work, I was brawling on the playground. The nun was disgusted and ordered my sister to take me to the back of the classroom and have a talk with me.

Beverly was weeping with humiliation. She was twelve years old and she had a filthy, bleeding little brother who mortified her. I quivered with shame as she wept and whispered, "Paul, please. You must be good." Her tears startled me. I remember she had no handkerchief, so dried her tears with her hair.

I tried to lay low. The classes were large and the nuns had little time and no patience for stragglers. A few were kindly, but others were volatile. In fourth grade I ignited sister Pancratius by fumbling at the blackboard with arithmetic problems. Suddenly she grabbed my hair and started banging my head on the board. To this day, the memory of her purple face astonishes me. It is magnified in my memory—the gray stubble on her quivering chin, her rimless glasses askew, the clacking of her heavy rosary as she slammed my head. When finally I cried, she stopped. But her anger did not subside. She went across the hall and fetched Sister Mary Joseph, who would be teaching me the next year.

"I want you to see what Paul Zimmer is doing," she said. She ordered me to work the problem again. "Show Sister what you are doing."

Once more I went through the whole miserable process of being incorrect in front of everyone. Bang. Sister Pancratius had me by the hair again, shaking my head like an apple in high wind. Even my piti-less classmates were horrified. Tough Gary Beadle said to me later, "If she grabs me like that, I'm going to be on her!" Sister Mary Joseph was appalled. Finally she grasped Pancratius's arm and restrained her. "Sis-ter, I don't think Paul is going to be able to do this today."

I was addled and lived in terror for weeks, but that day I at least learned *something*. I did not know about aging, abuse, celibacy, or meno-pause then; but I knew for certain that I was a screw up. I knew it that day, and I knew it for many days and years thereafter.

In high school I liked reading *Ivanhoe* and *Silas Marner* and *Julius Cae-sar*, in English class, but I drifted or sank in most other subjects. I looked intelligent and spoke well; I had a big head that seemed like it might be full of brains, but I was a prolific and unceasing daydreamer.

Beyond the sports leagues I played with paper cutouts of players, my most prominent fantasy was a diminutive town that I was going to create from balsam wood, toothpicks, and glue. I lulled myself in the classrooms and in bed at night by envisioning tiny neighborhoods—streets, alleys, garages, houses, sheds, groceries, church steeples rising over the rooftops, my electric train circling and bringing commerce to the little town. I would be mayor of this minute place, the headman in charge. When I had it built, I would open it to the public for viewing, sell tickets, make a fortune, and never have to have a job.

I bought supplies at a hobby shop and planned out the town on a slab of plywood in the basement. But I was a fumbling modeler. Once I showed one of my little houses to a neighbor lady. She looked away and said, "Ain't that teedjus!" I was not sure what she meant by this, but it gave me pause.

I slopped model dope over everything. My sponge bushes and baby's breath trees looked like clumps of mold. I never got my train wired properly to the platform. One bad day I looked at it all and admitted to myself that it was a dump, like something Elmer Fudd might have invented. I did not want to be boss of such a place. I tore it down, broke it up, and burned it in our trash barrel.

❧

In high school I failed algebra, Spanish, art (for God's sake!), Latin, and civics. I spent a lot of time struggling for Cs and Ds in make-up classes and finally graduated in the lower third of my class.

But the state of Ohio stipulated that anyone graduating from an Ohio high school must be permitted to enroll in a state college. My sister had gone to college and my parents felt that I might at last show some progress in the less regimented atmosphere of a university.

I went down like a stone again. I attended Kent State and lurched through a year. I failed English grammar twice, and the introductory courses to political science, sociology, psychology, and journalism. If a class bored me or puzzled me—and most of them did—I simply stopped attending. I had a great time drinking 3.2 beer, playing pool, and doing high jinx with my buddies.

For a while I had a girlfriend named Ginny, and we sought out dark corners of the campus for our hugging and kissing. One night we unwrapped from each other for a moment to catch our breath, and I was much emboldened and inspired.

"I wonder what your legs look like?"

Without hesitation Ginny reached down and pulled her skirt up to her thighs. There were her socks and saddle shoes, the white of her panties, and her gloriously turned legs in the moonlight. She held them out and spread them back and forth a bit so I could see them well. Once a boy had socked me in the solar plexus when I was not expecting it. It wasn't that pain I felt when Ginny showed me her legs, but the feeling that I might never be able to catch my breath again. The greatest daydream of all was coming into focus.

Being on my own at last, I felt sophisticated and adult. There were other girls and they were far more interesting than classes. I seemed to have a reality gap about school—a pattern of denial that I fell into again. In the back of my mind I knew what was coming at the end of the term, but pretended it was not going to happen. I daydreamed miracles, wonderful administrative mistakes in which good grades were given to me in error and I would be saved. I even imagined acts of benevolence from my professors, who would somehow recognize my great worth and give me passing grades. But I was at last banished from college, took a job in a steel mill, and then I was drafted.

In the army I told all my mates that I had gone to college. I did not fill in the details, but I was a *college* man and sought that status. My best buddies were graduates of Michigan, Purdue, Princeton, Stanford, Columbia, Oregon, Marquette. I hung around with them and listened to their talk about literature and ideas. I asked questions and read the books they loaned me. They were the first teachers I could relate to.

When I was discharged, I was eligible for the G.I. Bill and Kent permitted me to enroll again, but ruled that my old bad grades had to stand. Once again I was towing my atrocious deficit.

I had discovered poetry and fiction in the army and decided to devote myself to being a writer. I haunted the English department. The literature survey books only whetted my appetite. I wanted to read in depth the writers who attracted me. I scraped money from my G.I. Bill and a dishwashing job to buy the collected Yeats and Stevens, Modern Library or paperback editions of Hardy, Twain, Orwell, Dickinson, Whitman, the Brontes, Thoreau, Frost. I subscribed to *The Saturday Review of Literature*. Flannery O'Connor had recently published *A Good Man Is Hard to Find*, William Carlos Williams *The Desert Music*, Conrad Aiken *A Letter from Li Po*, Elizabeth Bishop *Poems: North and South, a Cold Spring*. I skipped some six-packs to afford these new books.

I read and read. I wanted to know why the whale was white. Where did the road not taken lead? Who was Ramon Fernandez? Why was Byzantium no place for old men? Why did Thoreau hate the railroad? I devoured books instead of textbooks. I did not always understand what I was reading—but that was part of my fascination. The clarity and confidence of these writers, the resonance of their cadence and tones drove me on through their mysterious, fascinating metaphors. I was dazzled by these articulate, sensuous people; they had the boldness to go beyond the mundane words of politicians, journalists, generals, teachers, clergymen, and entertainers. They made me feel things that were significant, human, and challenging. I wanted to extend myself in such a way, to devote my life to real words. It seemed to me to be the most important work in the world. None of this had anything to do with the drill of going to school: get in line, know your place, march, read the assignment, absorb the lectures, spout the answers. Good boy! Bad boy! Move on.

But I plugged away and usually attended my classes. Still, there were times when boredom overwhelmed me and I would falter. My most inventive and amazing excuse for my lapses came in my junior year when I actually made one of my fantasies come to life—I began writing a novel. This was an unusual activity for an undergraduate. One day I simply started writing, and the pile of pages mounted on my table. Of course it was halting, unpracticed work, but it gave me pride, and I began to think—by God, I am really going to be able to *do* this! I told all my professors that I had to devote myself to this artistic enterprise and felt that I was dealing with destiny. I willed them to believe that a novel in progress was more important than classes. I did not say it, but implied that they would not want to be known as the clueless teachers who had held back a Hemingway or Faulkner. They were all intrigued, at least by the ingenuity of my excuse, and a few of them even seemed sympathetic. But no one gave me anything I didn't earn.

Still, to my amazement, some English professors actually began to take an interest in me. They had me to their offices for chats. They even invited me to their homes and sat me down in comfortable chairs, played Bach fugues, Beethoven symphonies, Mozart quartets, Dylan Thomas and T. S. Eliot recordings. They read Shakespeare and Milton and Whitman and Yeats aloud to me. They showed me their treasured books. They invited me to dinner and gave me a good glass of wine to drink with wild rice and mushrooms, stroganoff and savory cheese. I listened to their wonderful talk. They asked me what I thought and when I realized that they were actually listening to my responses, I was elated. It was late, but not too late. With their encouragement, I rallied and almost graduated. But not quite.

Oh Lord! I needed a B in an American Cultural History course to bring my grade average up to the minimum for graduation. I had a B average on my tests and papers, but at the end of the term the professor gave me a C. I went to see him and explained my dilemma, describing the tortuous path I had taken to reach this point. He refused to change the grade, stating that I had not participated enough in classroom discussion. I told him I was going to be married in a month, was leaving the state to begin my life. He was not moved. Standards had to be maintained. I abruptly abandoned my formal education forever, and at last began to live my life.

Ten years later, I had published two well-reviewed books and was the associate director of a scholarly university press. An invitation came for me to read and lecture at Kent State and the publicity office wrote to say that they knew I had attended the university, but could not determine my year of graduation. So in 1969, at the age of thirty-five, ten years after I had stopped being formally educated, I was given an undergraduate college degree at a brief ceremony before my reading. It is my only honorary degree and I cherish it.

Why have I reconstructed these old miseries? Is it the urge to confess? Do I seek revenge? On whom? Dead nuns and professors? On life? My life went well enough after I left school. But when you consider that education is the center, the cornerstone of one's youth, my whole early life was a failure. I recall the loneliness and disgrace, the constant feelings of inadequacy. I deserve something for enduring this—perhaps if it is only to banish bad dreams.

Addendum: As our young people are sent into war, I think of my education again—back fifty years to when, for the first time ever, I was at last compelled by the army to focus on something and learn it completely. I later went to college on the G.I. Bill, but before this, the first thing my government taught me was to be a lethal human being. As a draftee I spent two months in basic training, then endured two additional months of organized mayhem called advanced combat infantry training.

Rifles, grenades, bazookas, machine guns, rocket launchers, mortars, hand-to-hand combat, flame-throwers, bayonets. My buddies and I were taught to be professional killers. Even at night, exhausted in our bunks, we fought phantom enemies in our dreams, until the cadre awakened us with insults at 5:00 A.M., and we resumed our mock annihilations.

It was like trying to make the football team. I was not very good at it—but I was good enough. I was a malleable nineteen-years old and my head was a void. Most of the college graduate draftees had gone on after initial basic training to specialty assignments in offices and commands, but the rest of us—mill-hands, farmers, ridge-runners, garage mechanics, laborers, janitors, dropouts, and flunkouts—went on to learn the finer points of death dealing.

The Korean War had ended, but the Cold War had commenced, and there were possibilities of police actions in Lebanon and other "hot spots." We were assured that we might yet have our opportunity, our crack at some real enemies. Tough on the surface, we privately wondered whether we could actually practice what we had learned. Would we be brave under fire? Could we kill the enemy?

At the end of our strenuous days we talked the earnest blather of young men in the barracks:

"What are you thinking about, Weiss?"

"My girlfriend's brassiere. The night before I left for this Goddamned hole, I finally learned how to unhook it."

"Too late."

"Naw. It wasn't too late. But that's all I got on my mind now. What else is there to think about in this place?"

"Sergeant Moulds's breath in your face."

"I'd rather smell the latrine."

"Hey, Stanfield. Why'd you fall out today going up Misery Hill?"

"I wasn't feeling so good."

"You were fakin', man."

"You won't be fakin' no fall if you say that again, motherfucker!"

"Hey! Come on, you guys! We start to fighting each other, we won't have nothing left for the Russians. You looked good today on the range, Stanfield. Nine bulls. Not too bad."

"Thanks, man."

I think back to that young man sitting on his bunk, cleaning his rifle. All the cells in my body have changed many times since then. I have lived a long time, done good work and bad work. I ask myself, would I have killed other men for my country? My response is like a jagged piece of ice lodged in my memory. Yes. Yes, probably I would have. I had at last been taught something completely—to be manly and cruel. An unsentimental education. I had nothing else in my mind.

Eventually I was assigned to do other work in the army, but at that time the physical part of my life overwhelmed the mental and spiritual.

We used to chuckle when Sergeant Moulds said, "You better give your souls to God, because your asses belong to me." But he meant it. I think of the young people now, sweating it out, giving their souls to God, not having lived their lives yet.

Part Two ∾

I would there were no age between sixteen and
three-and-thirty, or that youth would sleep out
the rest; for there is nothing in the between
but getting wenches with child, wronging the
ancientry, stealing, fighting.
   —William Shakespeare, *The Winter's Tale*

Lovely Muck

Uncle Coon Cable was not really my uncle, but my father's ne'er-do-well cousin. After brief success as a local semiprofessional baseball player in the early 1930s, Uncle Coon had descended, without any other skills, into the bar life. Over the years he had lost most of his teeth and his false ones pinched him, so he kept them in his shirt pocket. He gummed chewing tobacco and looked like an ancient lizard. Folks still liked to stand drinks for old Coon, remembering the pleasure he had given them as a pitcher. He had no money for his room in a boarding house, so my dad helped by hiring him to do odd jobs around our house.

Uncle Coon was not a dedicated worker; he had lost his job as a gandy dancer for the railroads years before. I was fascinated by him and followed him around as he mowed the grass and hacked at our bushes. I noticed one day he was making frequent trips down into our basement. Dad had learned how to make home brew during Prohibition, and he still occasionally put up batches in the cellar. Uncle Coon had hidden a tin cup on a nail up in the rafters and I found him slurping the still-working beer—wretched, horrid-smelling stuff.

"Dad says that won't be right for a while," I told him.

"Oh, it's good enough as it is," Uncle Coon said. "It's hot out there and I get thirsty."

By the time Dad came home from work Uncle Coon had taken hold of the clothesline in the backyard with one hand and was flapping and swaying like a dirty shirt, blathering a strange language to himself. Dad took him around the corner of the house where they had a long, loud talk. Uncle Coon had to take a nap for a while on the front porch glider, then Mom made him some sandwiches and Dad walked him to the bus stop.

I asked dad later what had been wrong with Uncle Coon, and he looked at me carefully. "Well," he said. "You should know this, I guess. He was what they call drunk. He had too much of the beer. It made him sick."

"Will he be all right?"

"Not if he keeps doing things like that. Some people have trouble with that sort of thing. They drink too much beer and it makes them silly. It's kind of sad."

My old drinking buddies. The five of us were callow and rudimentary, but we learned how to drink beer together. Ohio served 3.2 percent beer to eighteen-year-olds in those days, but we found dim, out-of-the-way bars that did not check I.D.s and managed to get started when we were seventeen. The drafts cost a dime and if we drank until our kidneys groaned, spending not much more than a buck, we could get a fair buzz on. We felt very adult, sitting at the bars or jammed into a booth together. The most sophisticated, important moment in our day came when we were deciding which tavern to begin our swilling in. Usually we went on until we were totally sodden.

Our talk was the ardent, innocent chat of young men. Sometimes we envisioned what we would do with our lives. Austin said he wanted to be a clown, and was always breaking us up with his pratfalls. He planned to become so good, he would never have to take off his makeup. He would be a clown all the time. Beany was our best athlete and was going to be a professional second baseman. Chase had given up even thinking about anything else—he was just going to be a bartender. Tucker said he wanted to be a preacher because they only had to work one day a week. We got a honk out of that, but he really meant it. When I said I wanted to be a poet, they laughed about that. But I really meant it, too.

Austin spoke for all of us one night during one of our more muted discussions after half a dozen rounds. "I'd just like to stay slightly loaded all the time," he said.

There *was* that moment of light clarity and pleasantness that comes in the early stages of drinking alcohol—but we never lingered there. We hastened past it to begin the slow slide down into earnest blather, then incoherence.

"You ready for another?"

"Yeah."

We had come into a general stupor one evening, grown numb and silent together, when Austin asked artlessly of us all, "When are you an alcoholic?" This surprised us. It was a daunting question. We had all secretly thought about it at one time or another, but Austin, having thrown it out for discussion, threw us into deeper silence as we hazily searched for an answer. Finally Chase offered, "My Uncle Schleig says it's when you stop getting hangovers that you need to start worrying."

Lord, we were such naives, so hapless where we sat in the tacky, hacked-up booth! We actually felt relieved by Tucker's response. Yes, all of us felt wretched in the mornings, but now we could feel grateful for our misery.

I was the literary member of the group. Occasionally after dinner, before heading out to meet my pals in the bars, I would read a bit. One evening I brought along my copy of "A Shropshire Lad" and read to them:

> Oh I have been to Ludlow fair
> And left my necktie God knows where,
> And carried half way home or near,
> Pints and quarts of Ludlow beer:
> Then the world seemed none so bad,
> And I myself a sterling lad;
> And down in lovely muck I've lain,
> Happy till I woke again.
> Then I saw the morning sky:
> Heighho, the tale was all a lie;
> The world, it was the old world yet,
> I was I, my things were wet,
> And nothing now remained to do
> But begin the game anew.

Tucker had taken a few world history courses in high school. He deemed this our magna carta and we all memorized it, as we memorized the lyrics of jump tunes like "How High the Moon" or "Honeysuckle Rose," which we intoned as we blearily drove to the next tavern.

It was Beany's car. He was a sweet, earnest young man whose life had been broken by domestic violence and divorce. By way of trying to make up for things, Beany's father bought him a second-hand Ford coupe. It was the first car owned by anyone in our group, and it became our official vehicle. We all bought trimmings for it—foam-rubber dice, monkey jigglers, and plastic bikini girls. Beany unscrewed the old gear-shift knob and hammered a Budweiser draft handle onto the shaft. We stuffed ourselves into that little car and rode it like a chariot to the taverns, sometimes at the peril of our lives.

Beany had been deeply scarred. Sometimes, after drinking for a while, he would want to hit someone or something—fortunately never one of us. But if another group of young men taunted us, Beany was first to accept the challenge, drawing us into the scuffle, which generally ended up in the parking lot with bloody noses and some wrestling in the gravel. "Fuck you!" we shouted at each other when it started, and "Fuck you!" when it was over; then we would go back into the tavern to wash our wounds with another round.

But usually Beany did not pick fights; he'd smash something with his fist—a jukebox, a men's room soap dish, or even a plate glass window. Then we would all run to pile into his coupe and roar off, gasping and giggling, ducking into another tavern for sanctuary and another round. Beany wrapped his hand in his handkerchief and we went on soaking up draught.

The next day he would be appalled with himself. I could not persuade him that his apologies were unnecessary. Sometimes Beany would say he wanted to kill his old man. He was afraid for himself when he said this, and his fear infected us all. What would become of us?

We tried to imagine the future—and the future always included alcohol. All of us wanted to slip into some easy-living situation. Each of us would nail down a quick million or two apiece, then take it soft the rest of our lives. We would live in mansions near one another, have bars in our recreation rooms, and get together most nights for some drinks before going home to make love to our wives.

When I received my draft notice almost fifty years ago, I was disconsolate. My uncle, who had served in World War II and been through the whole drill, took me aside. "The army isn't much fun, but look upon this as an opportunity. You're going to see new places. Don't just hang around in bars when you're on pass. Go to museums and parks and concerts. Go to bookstores. This doesn't have to be wasted time. Learn something."

But I was an unpracticed, thin-minded kid. Of course, the first thing I did when I got off base was head for a tavern and fall face-first into a glass of beer. Then and now, there are assuredly saintly, motivated young people in the world, but I was not one of them.

Morning sunlight pried my eyes open and blared into my throbbing skull. I was sprawled in the backseat of a strange car amongst tacky Styrofoam cups and soiled paper napkins. My mouth tasted like a raided bird's nest. My gorge rose, then settled back down my throat.

My wits began to blink back on painfully through the nausea. Pain rumbled behind my eyeballs. Where was I? I had no idea. Whose vehicle was this? How had I come to be here? I had no recollection—but I had to get out of the strange car. It was early morning and there was no one about. I pushed the door open and lurched onto the concrete.

Surf sounds and ocean breezes swept up over the descending rooftops through distant palm fronds to cool the sweat of my head. I took a few steps, then had to lean against a fender. The houses were pink and yellow stucco. There were sprinklers on in some of the yards and rainbows in the spray over the dichondra. Bougainvillea clawed up trellises around the walls. A dog barked at me through a curtained Spanish window. Gulls were flocking and fussing over distant beaches.

My mind began lurching painfully back into place. Then I remembered. Los Angeles. I was in Los Angeles. I had come on leave with some friends from our army base in Nevada. How had I come to be in the car? The toes of my shoes were scraped as if I had been dragged, and one knee of my khakis was soiled and torn. I had never felt so wretched. How had I come to such a thing?

I had done it again, deliberately drunk my brains out. But this time, frighteningly, there was a hole in my memory of the previous night, and the thought of it made my gorge rise again.

We had started making the bars along the beaches. I was still not even a legal drinker, but I wore a uniform. We were glad to be away from the miserable, isolated army camp, had walked the sand most of the afternoon, ogling beautiful women in bathing suits. We were happy, titillated by the beach crowd. As always, I drank a bit more than everyone else. I believed it was the sophisticated thing to do, and had learned early how to drink. Besides, I was going to be a writer. Many of my heroes—Edgar Allen Poe, Dylan Thomas, Ernest Hemingway, Thomas Wolfe, William Faulkner, jazz musicians like Charlie Parker, Lester Young, Coleman Hawkins—were legendary boozers.

But after my initial elation in the bars, I had no recollection of what had happened to me. It was terrifying. Apparently I had been non compos mentis and must have fallen down. It seemed that someone had dragged me to an unlocked car and shoved me in, rather than leave me collapsed on the street. There were bumps on the side of my head and cheek. Had there been a fight? My God! In the whole lushy, neon city of Los Angeles, that night I must have had the distinction of being the most intoxicated person.

Shakespeare observes that a drunkard is "Like a drown'd man, a fool, and a madman: one draught above heat makes him a fool; the second mads him, and a third drowns him." I had not yet quite drowned—but had gone past the madman and was headed into the deep surf.

Fortunately, I never went permanently under the waves. The gap in my consciousness in Los Angeles frightened me into making serious adjustments. I went on in my dogged way, finding other ways to reward myself, and carefully managing my shortcomings. Good sense about alcohol never came easily to me, and occasionally I dared this tendency—but by the grace of some god, I did not end up babbling and hanging from a clothesline with one hand.

Some people seem more inclined to the bottles than others. Most writers I know enjoy having a drink or two or three. There seems to exist a provisional kinship between alcohol and the writing craft—a sort of reward and support earned after serious probing of the psyche with words, a release from the tension of writing. Booze rarely seems to give direct aid to the ongoing creative process—I have known only a few writers who write as they drink—but it rewards the process when it is completed, relaxing and staging the writer for further work. It gives license to a range a bit beyond what one has comfortably arranged for oneself. It is a form of celebration for work, an excuse to ease up a bit on the controls, an easement of routine that can sometimes furnish insights that would not ordinarily be available. It does provide a mild Rimbaudian derangement of the senses, but it does not seem to provide "vision"—perhaps the illusion of vision, which offers possibilities that sometimes can be useful in writing. It also tends to give the delusion of profundity, promoting a kind of overconfidence that can be harmful. More often than I care to think about, carried too far, it has caused me to become a silly, incoherent man.

Suzanne and I have had a late afternoon ritual for years. Around 5:30 we come in from whatever we are doing; I bring out bottles and glasses, Suzanne brings snacks, and we sit down for our drink together. We look forward to this daily ritual, are pleasantly altered by it, chatting for a while—or just sitting together quietly to enjoy our sip.

Things are delicately suspended, reality briefly postponed, and there is an undeniable warmth and conviviality, a small celebration to look forward to at the end of each day. We do not extend this custom. Too much is too much, and what comes after too much is rarely worthwhile or constructive.

I will not be smug about this civility. Luck and resolve brought me to it. I still maintain a healthy fear of what could send me back into the sullen taverns and under the waves for good. Loss, loneliness, sickness, indigence, anger, deterioration. I hope for courage and good fortune.

The year before I left the University of Iowa, Suzanne and I sold our house in Iowa City and temporarily moved to an apartment in the student district. It was one of the more ill-considered mistakes of my advancing years. I have lived in college towns for forty years and have helped raise two children, so I felt that I was in reasonable touch with young people. But I had distanced myself from youth. Even if I had been the coolest old man in town, I was not ready for this experience.

Every night young people babbled in loud glossolalia outside our window. In the apartment I pulled the covers over my head, but I had no place to hide and had aged beyond patience. Shame on me. I recollected my own staggering youth, how prodigiously the suds went down, but these blathering youths vexed me. They were a torment, and seemed like some form of long-delayed penance.

I found these exasperated lines the other day, scrawled in a notebook I kept at that time:

How to Be Young

Have a fistfight in the street at three in the morning.
Shout loudly outside the nearest open window.
Say that everything sucks. Make your car
Throb like a giant tom-tom in the dark.
Freeze your pizza barf in the snow.
Wear your baseball cap backwards.
Roll your empties down the gutter.

I had become a scowling geezer walking my dog in the streets. To my small credit, if these young people had paused to speak to me, I would have tried to give them good counsel. But they hurried by as if I was a gray ghost, as if they knew what I would say to them and did not want to hear it.

"Don't drown," I would have cautioned. "Don't hang on clotheslines. Stay out of the lovely muck."

William Metts, American Poet

A husky, crewcut gnome was stepping it off alone in the middle of the midnight street, chanting:

> *Your left, your left,*
> *Your left, right, left.*
> *Hambone, hambone, where you been?*
> *Down in old town drinkin' gin.*
> *Am I right or wrong?*
> *Am I right or wrong?*

The singular apparition marched his invisible company with precision and vigor. I had been lurching home from an evening of beer and talk with friends, and stepped into a store doorway to watch him stride past and turn down Franklin Avenue:

Column right! March!

I crept back and turned the corner to watch. He was a small man, looming large as he swaggered under the streetlights. His spectral troop seemed in fine whack as he marched them past the dilapidated train station.

In the mid-fifties only a few passenger trains still passed through Kent, Ohio, slow runs that ended up in big cities like Pittsburgh and Cleveland. The Erie Station was skeletal and grungy. In an unmowed patch of weeds stood a weather-beaten World War II honor board of men who had served from Kent. Some of the nameplates had slipped and were hanging by one screw, but the diminutive drill sergeant commanded his troops:

Eyes—left!

and he snapped his right hand up to his brow in a trig salute. Another block down, in front of the Rathskeller bar he brought his heels together:

> *Company, halt!*
> *Oh-rder arms.*
> *Pah-rade rest.*
> *At ease, men.*
> *Smoke 'em if you've got 'em.*

The sergeant went into the bar for another beer, leaving his phantom troops at ease in the autumnal fog. He couldn't have been much more than an inch over minimum service height, but his stride was long and authoritative to match that of larger men. As he walked into the tavern I could see by the neon lights that his brush cut head was large on his compact body, his nose was blunt, his blue eyes were quick and acute. Even in the chill, he had his muscular forearms uncovered and they were tattooed with marine eagles.

I had heard of Bill Metts from other students. That was the first time I saw him. I was not likely to forget. I had learned to be wary of drill sergeants, and I could see that, even though this man was only slightly over five feet in height, he was not to be trifled with. He was a legend amongst the artistic types at Kent State in the mid-fifties, a red-blooded writer whose work was published regularly in the student magazine. Just back from military service myself, I was in awe of him and diffident. He seemed so inventive and unpredictable.

Some of us literary types gathered on warm evenings with six-packs of beer at a place we referred to as "under the bridge" on the banks of the Cuyahoga River near the Main Street bridge. Across the river were train tracks and we watched the doomed steam engines and new diesels rumble through, pulling boxcars of big city freight, their lamps flashing in the currents of the river as we talked and recited, dreaming of our writing careers in the enchanted East or West. Metts joined the group a few times when I was there and was immediately the center of attention. I believe he knew who I was, but he did not speak to me. I had not earned my stripes yet. I sat away from him and kept my mouth shut. He had amazing, on-your-toes, Cagney-like energy, knew many lines of poetry by heart—Whitman, Keats, Tennyson, Milton, Wordsworth, Housman. He recited vividly on the dark riverbank and we all grew quiet as he rolled out the lines in his deep voice. He said his own poems sometimes, too, and I greatly admired his intensity and the passion he felt for words. We were all beginners, but I felt that if any of us were going to make it, it would be Metts.

In those salad days I inevitably carried a book under my arm, with the title out so my friends would be impressed with the cool stuff I was reading. It was my writer's badge. I was scoping the downtown scene one evening with an impressive tome under my arm when Metts came with a crony down the street the other way. I could see he was not in a good mood and probably drunk. I had heard he was losing out with his beautiful girlfriend. I knew the guy he was with and nodded as we passed. Metts curled his lip; he had little use for pretension. He reached out and knocked my copy of *The Flowers of Evil* to the pavement. When I retrieved it, I looked back angrily and my acquaintance was shaking his head. No, no. Metts trudged on. What was I going to do anyway? Go back and strap-on to this disgruntled ex-marine? I would have lost teeth.

Years later, I ran into him by chance when we were both living in California. It took us a while to become good friends. I was still wary of him, and he wasn't sure he could trust anyone who wore a coat and tie. But we both trusted poetry. One day I teased him about the time he knocked the book out of my arm. He did not remember the incident, but he grew terribly upset. I had to assure him that I had long ago forgiven him, but he remained chagrined. I attempted to change the subject, but he wouldn't let go.

"Did I *really* do that?" His head was hanging. "My God! I was always pulling that Marine Corps, tough guy shit!" he said in despair.

"Hey, pal, come on, that was years ago. We were just kids."

"I'm lucky to have lived through my childhood," he said inconsolably.

We got together in California as often as we could. I worked for a book distributor and had an office. Metts had fallen in with a group of easy-going people in the Sierra Madre hills. He wore sandals and lived hand-to-mouth. Both of us worked constantly at our poems. When I went to visit him I had to knock on many doors. His friends and neighbors were guarded. Anyone wearing a suit and straw hat had to be the fuzz or a bill collector. But I was dogged and persuasive. One old man, a drinking buddy of Bill's, came to his door with a quart of Thunderbird in hand. He scowled at me as if I was a leper.

"I ain't seen Bill in months," he said. "He must have gone away." His beard was gray and he drooled and spattered as he spoke, but he remembered his manners and raised his jug to my face. "You want a pull?"

Women were attracted to Bill and, in those early days, he gave as many as possible full opportunity to enjoy his attentions. I recall one enraptured young woman telling me that she had purchased a lifetime subscription to *Time* because Bill had told her that someday he was going to be on the cover.

I came to the hills one day to visit Bill and, after some probing, his reticent friends finally informed me that he had fallen off a roof and been badly hurt. I drove to the veteran's hospital in Long Beach and found him lying in traction, his head turned in despair, gazing across the ward at the top of an ailanthus tree outside the far window. He had broken his back; there would be no more marching for Bill. When he saw me he regained himself.

"How are your poems?" he asked.

"I'm still hammering," I said. "What have you done to yourself?"

"Too much booze and stargazing. I fixed myself up pretty good." A stretcher rolled down the aisle, its wheels wobbly and squeaking. In a distant ward someone was shouting over and over. Bill lifted his big, rugged, close-cropped head and recited Byron:

> For the sword outwears its sheath,
> And the soul wears out the breast,
> And the heart must pause to breathe,
> And love itself have rest.

Though the night was made for loving,
And the day returns too soon,
Yet we'll go no more a roving
By the light of the moon.

Bill's ward mates had grown used to his declamations. They smiled
and looked over from their beds when he began, but my tears made
them turn their heads away.

Bill began his new life as a paraplegic in a wheelchair. It is hard for me
to think of the agonies of spirit and body, of the resentment and terror
he must have suffered in coming to terms with his broken lower half,
so important to any man, but especially to Bill. But he went on. He
married a beautiful, felicitous woman named Susan and they lived in a
small house in the desert near Victorville. In the late sixties I moved
east for a job and our meetings became rare, but we remained steadfast
and regularly exchanged letters and poems. Occasionally I would see
him when I made trips to the West.

With Susan's help, he settled resolutely into his life in the desert.
He took up woodworking and stonecutting, creating handsome objects, and every day he worked at his poems. He obtained a telescope
and spent many nights scanning the clear, desert skies. His letters were
full of planet watching, galaxies, and star clusters. Over the years he
took astronomical photographs. I keep on my desk a moon image and
one of his wondrous views of the Hale-Bopp comet. Earthbound in his
wheelchair, he dreamed of flying, studied books on aircraft and read
the biographies of the great fliers.

In the late 1970s he and Susan came in their specially outfitted van
to visit us for a few days in Pittsburgh. We lived in an old city neighborhood built over a western Pennsylvania ridgetop, and our house
was up thirty steps. Susan and I eased and tugged Bill's wheelchair up
the steps one-by-one.

It always heartens and instructs me to think how brave and uncom-
plaining Bill was when he was most vulnerable. To be hauled around
was agony for him, but he kept his head up and teased us as we struggled
on the steps with his chair. When it was time for them to go a few days

later, we realized that easing Bill back down in his chair would be even more dangerous and frightening to him. Finally Susan figured out that I could tote him down on my back like a fireman.

Neither Bill nor I looked forward to this. We decided to do it in the early morning, so not to provide a spectacle for the neighbors. Bill had very strong arms and he wrapped them around my neck from behind. As I descended with him clinging to my back I knew he was fearful that we would both go plunging headlong down the cement steps; but partway down he growled in my ear, softly so our worried wives would not hear, half in despair and half in high humor, "Oh, man, don't you just love buggery?" I wavered with my load, but made it the rest of the way down.

On one of our California visits in the early 1990s he arranged an early morning trip to a place near Edwards Air Force Base where a space shuttle was due to land. We wheeled him into a clearing and watched with him the astonishing spectacle of the shuttle suddenly plunging into view like a great bird out of the blue, then gliding serenely down into the base beyond the hills. We were all agog, but Bill was exhilarated, transported by the sight of this marvelous passage.

A few years ago they came to our Wisconsin farm. I wanted to show Bill some of our fields and have him look into our woods, so I devised a way to roll his wheelchair up onto our tractor wagon and secure it with bungee cords. I could tell he still felt insecure, so I tied a rope to the tractor seat and he hung on with both hands as we rolled around on the bumpy fields.

Susan took a picture of us with Bill's camera: I am smiling my snapshot smile on the tractor seat, but Bill, mounted on the wagon, is looking off, his knuckles white on the rope, like paintings of Napoleon slumped on his charger at Waterloo.

My friend is gone now. I miss his words, his images, the poems we read to each other, his wonderful talk, the wine and beer we drank together, his loving counsel, his wit and sensitivity.

Bill Metts trusted the process and language of poetry. He gave every day of his adult life, much of his body and spirit to his practice with what he called "the holy words." He loved Shakespeare and Chaucer and John Donne, but he distrusted contemporary poetry. Probably his distaste was grudging, although as far as I know, he rarely tried to publish or gain notice. He had no airs and he had the rectitude not to complain about his condition or his obscurity. Like most poets, he was waiting to be discovered, but this never happened.

He had his own view of the process: You decide you want to be a poet and you realize you must give your life to it. You write the best poems you can. "Not every carpenter drives a nail the same way," he said, "and not all of them build the Taj Mahal." Poetry was not a workshop. When I sent him critical comments on his work, he ignored them. He wanted me to praise his poems, not pick at them. This was what it was *about*—praise for the spirit of this work he did in his remote desert home, for the act itself, the longing it expressed, the compassion, the loneliness, and the holiness. It was his miracle, that he had come to this, that he could write these words. They were his view, his charge, and they were not for piddling and carping. And so I praised him, showed appreciation for his short, crafted poems about large subjects: stars, stones, sun, earth, love, sky, death, planets, time. He did not agree when I suggested that he bring his focus down to concentrate on smaller things, which would ultimately represent larger topics with more intensity. He teased me in a poem:

> Zimmer broke out the beer and we drank
> and talked about Big Stuff:
> Supernovas, Freedom, Women, Poetry
> and the Cubs.

And we did that, sometimes sopping up more than we should have in the process, reading out loud to each other the great poems on big subjects—Wordsworth on immortality, Whitman on America, Emily Dickinson on death, Shakespeare on love—marveling and chuckling to each other until our wives prevailed at a late hour and made us retire.

In his writing Bill always went straight to the target, as he had done when he was a combat marine. Occasionally he referred to this experience in his poems, but he did not whimper or become gaunt. In his poem, "Winter Reunion," he regards the "earth betonned / with snow" and thinks:

> In some such chilly bed, soldiers
> I have slain are frozen in
> the memory of their last
> ungainly fall.

He calls them brothers and wishes he could sit and drink with them quietly, as together they regard the chinaberry in his yard. They were his demon phantoms, too. He was a child of our warlike tribe and of an era when we fought four wars, and he did what he was ordered to do. He had felt great fear, and he had killed many enemies. It was what he had been taught.

He was a tough man, sometimes mistaken, sometimes misbehaving, but he was not long-suffering. He had come close to becoming a lost person when he was young, before his accident, but I do not believe that his accident "tamed" him. It compelled him to focus his tremendous energy and it brought to the fore his inherent civility. He would have been a poet in any event. As it was, he stretched his life and took the blows fairly. He grew to gentleness and wisdom through his poems, and he was aware that they were the source of his spirit.

His poems are the work of a man who lived his poetry and abidingly loved words, a man who was reverent in the face of nature and large in his utterance and perception of the human experience. Most of all, his poems were written out of the tremendous responsibility he felt as a poet in an indifferent world. They are not just snappy, conversational exercises or grand lists—and they are not the work of a writer who is trying to ingratiate or impress readers with flashy intellect.

Bill Metts did not know any of the "correct" people—nor, indeed, would they have wanted to know him. He wasn't their type. He was, as one famous poet once said to me about another lesser brother, "without consequence."

But Bill Metts endured his last thirty-five years in a wheel chair in great consequence, working on his poems, creating beautiful objects, gazing at the stars, and rolling himself through the sand around his desert house in California. He lived with varying degrees of pain and physical difficulties. For periods of time he had to check into the veterans' hospital in Long Beach. He complained rarely, but occasionally he longed in his poems:

> I remember when these
> veins sang;
> when the muscles clasped
> stone bones, and
> dead weight clutched at Earth
> in vain against a back
> whose spring was
> hickory.

He far exceeded the expectations of his doctors and friends, but at the end he injured himself again, things got worse, there were amputations, even more complications arose and he had a major crisis. But he willed himself to rally, and got home to spend some last, brief days with Susan. She sent a snapshot—Bill is lying on his stomach on a padded platform laid across his wheelchair. He has his head up and Susan is squatting close beside him. Both of them are grinning in unabashed happiness to be together. There was "lots of face kissing" Bill wrote to me. Then it was back to the ward.

Even in his last excruciating days in the hospital he worked at lines scrawled on a journal pad as he lay face down in his agony, going to the well one last time. He refers to himself as a battlefield. "There is more and more and more, and less to fight with." Perhaps he was recalling the fear he felt as a young man, facing the night attacks of shrieking, bell-ringing waves of Chinese Communist troops—scenes he had suppressed, but now felt these phantoms washing over him in his final suffering and dying. Still, face down in torment, he worked at his lines:

PAIN MEDS WEAR OFF

watch correct at midnight
when the howling comes

think of me
when the howling comes
in the night
yes think of me
that is me there
howling

Susan sent a note from the hospital. They had gone from "cure" to "comfort measures only." Bill had been given to his dying. "Now he can soar among the stars, moon, planets and out to other galaxies," she wrote.

Yes, I think of him as flying. I do not think of him in pain. I remember him as a poet, the unlikeliest and bravest poet I have known. No pretender or slacker, he was a man who became wise enough in time, rising out of unceasing difficulties to sustain himself with the holy words, in a small corner of the planet, where it really matters.

Mon Dentiste

Thy teeth are like a flock of sheep that are even
shorn, which came up from the washing.
      —Song of Solomon, 4:1

Wisconsin Public Radio features "Talk that matters to you." One morning I was jerked awake by an evangelistic voice on the clock radio—a
monologue from an impassioned dentist. I am vulnerable at cockcrow
before I have tea. In the state between dreams and chill early reality I
might believe anything. According to this dental partisan, the spiritual center of our lives is the aura surrounding molars, incisors, canines, and bicuspids. There might be other concerns and difficulties
in life, but when the cards are all out on the table everything comes
down to our teeth.

He made it sound as if my cogs were more important than my heart.
Listening to his exuberance, it seemed plausible. He claimed that if I
flossed carefully a couple of times a day it would add six years to my
life. It was more necessary than exercise or proper diet. Removal of
plaque seemed more important than breathing. It cut the risk of infections and removed harmful wee beasties from my body. I ran the tip of
my tongue over the skin of my morning teeth and felt guilty. I have
always resisted reality when it comes to my teeth. I did not wish to be
challenged this way at 6:30 in the morning.

Teeth can get the best of you, can almost possess your life. I once
knew a jazz musician who was the son of a dentist. He lived the midnight life and enjoyed it, but he had bad teeth and felt great guilt
about them. They were always at the forefront of his consciousness.
When he missed a brushing his father complex got the best of him,

and he felt ill at ease. When they flared up he couldn't play. When they weren't giving him fits he worried anyway, anticipating their next assault. He was a moody fellow. I asked him why he brooded all the time and he was disbelieving.

"My fangs, man," he responded with wariness, as if he could not fathom the stupidity of such a question. "Teeth!"

Old Doc Rubright was the beast of my Saturday mornings. While other children played happily, I had to take an early bus through streets of gray snow all the way across town with a bunch of hacking elders to his dreary office in a medical building. There was always a wait, and by early spring I had read and reread many times the dog-eared Christian comic books in his waiting room. I often considered playing hooky, but his receptionist was an unsmiling bird dog and without hesitation would have reported me to my parents.

My front adult incisors had grown in slightly askew. Doc Rubright worked with a form of cheap orthodontia—removable braces, which he built like partial denture plates with wires so they could be slipped off easily for cleaning. Because they weren't mounted permanently, they had to be regularly adjusted and tightened.

My wife, Suzanne, a properly modest person, tells me that when she was a little girl she once bit a dentist—hard—when he tried to stick a Novocain needle into her gums, then dashed from his office with him in hot pursuit. "He was very angry," she says, and to this day she is not certain what he would have done had not her mother intervened. She sustains an earned, intelligent wariness of dentists to this day.

Old Doc Rubright bore down on me every week, his stubby fingers in my mouth, his breath rank with coffee, all his bestial, wicked tools lined up in racks and trays within full sight—prickers, huge pliers, knives, pokers, gouges, chisels, mallets. His menacing drill perched like a corded pterodactyl just to the right of my head, ready to fly into torturous action. While my friends were romping in the Saturday leaves or having snow ball fights, Doc Rubright tilted me back, shined his bright light in my eyes, said, "Open wide," and stuck chill, pointed things in my mouth. *Every* Saturday. I looked into his eyes and waited for his sentence. Very early on in our relationship he'd given up trying to be jolly with me. He no longer chuckled at my naive questions, but grimly ignored them or responded crisply like a priest from the confessional.

"Tch-tch," he'd say. "I *wish* you would brush." I looked at the reflection of my frightened, anxious little face in his glasses, then I'd look up past the pinholes of light shining through the mat of his gray toupee, out his dingy window to where some filthy pigeons roosted in the icy drain of a building across the street. They seemed as miserable as I was.

On good days he merely adjusted and tightened the braces, but often enough I had to pay further penance. "We're going to work on that cavity," he'd say, as if it was a group effort. He always started before the Novocain took full effect, and his drill ran at the speed of frigid water slowly twirling down a drain. There was a nasty smell of decayed dust. My eyes watered. It went on and on. He'd stop, give me a paper cup of water to rinse with, then peer into my mouth. I'd gaze up into the hairy darkness of his nostrils and pray—but nobody was listening. He'd swing the drill back into my face and go on. In the end he mixed a little mound of silver filling compound on his tray, brought it in tiny scoops to my tooth, and packed it crunching and squeaking into the little hole as if he were filling a pothole.

He specialized in torturing little boys. It was always exactly noon when he finished working on me. "Don't eat or drink anything for two hours," he said as he put on his jacket to go out for lunch, and my stomach would moan and gurgle.

After a month the filling fell out. "Tch-tch," Doc Rubright said and back flew the pterodactyl into my face.

I was famous in grade school for having a removable brace and had to demonstrate frequently for groups of admirers. It was one of my few distinctions while I attended St. John's. Often I removed the brace and slipped it into my shirt pocket. Once I lost it and spent two terrified, lonely days keeping my mouth closed at home, and searching in secret over the park field where I had been playing football. Eventually I found it, but my incisors are still slightly crooked.

Dick Schiavone was one of my great boyhood friends. He was clever, loyal, athletic, inventive, handsome, and very intelligent. His only fault, as far as I was concerned, was that he wanted to be a dentist. It

63

seemed an inordinate desire. Schiavone, my noble friend, who shared great adventures with me, who stuck with me through the triumph and pain of boyhood, wanted to become one of those monsters! I could not comprehend his strange ambition.

Unlike me, he was an excellent student. I knew that dental school was challenging, requiring more discipline and intelligence than I could ever dream of. But if old Doc Rubright could make it through, so could my friend, Schiavone. I knew that dentists made very good livings and, as Schiavone pointed out, relieved suffering and helped people to be healthy. Still, they made people groan and children cry. They caused me the most pain I had felt in my life.

But if Schiavone wanted to do this, it was all right. He went off to dental school at Ohio State, and I bombed out of Kent State after a year, went to work in a steel mill until it went on strike, then was drafted into the army. After this, I became a poet. Talk about inordinate desire! Talk about numbness and the drill!

There is an uneasy, almost sensual intimacy in dental work—the nearness, the unwonted proximity; normally, we don't allow people to get this close to us without feeling affection for them. We have an aversion to strangers touching us, especially our face. Dentistry violates our privacy. It is almost voyeuristic. You reveal things when you yawn your mouth open to another person's touch and gaze. You open your head and expose some of its secrets—habits bad or good, matters of health, diet, care, and neglect. The flaws in our teeth hold durable stories—when a person's body is burned or maimed beyond recognition, they are identified by their teeth.

Dr. Victoria Plum was a handsome, dark-haired woman. Because of her commitments she had to cancel my appointment for a root canal and now, as I was due to leave on a trip, she rescheduled for a Saturday morning when her staff was off. I had a sense of déjà vu—Doc Rubright Saturdays. But this was a little different. It was a matter of expediency. And if you are going to be trapped on a Saturday morning with a dentist—much better with Victoria Plum than old Doc Rubright. She assured me that she had done this many times, had learned how to work by herself when she was in dental school.

Perhaps she had not eaten breakfast or was on a diet, for when she began concentrating on her work, her stomach pressed against my ear and she gurgled loudly. When she stepped away to fetch a tool or study my x-rays I could hear her effervescing in the distance.

It was bewitching. I couldn't wait for her to return to my side. It went on and on. Growrr, went her stomach. Rrrrufff. I forgot that I was uncomfortable. She knew I was listening. Some of her own secrets were being revealed. I couldn't escape or make a polite remark, and she had no choice but to go on with her work. I was too old to be noticeably aroused by her internal murmuring, but it was . . . fascinating, right up against my ear. If I had been forty years younger with raging hormones I would have been in serious difficulty.

The fact that she was drilling, manipulating, sliding things in and out of my head in the quiet solitude of her office added to the effect. I have been damnably straight all my life. I did not even presume to think of hanky panky, and she was concentrating on nothing else but my tooth, but somehow, with the furnace sighing, water gurgling in her sink, and her tummy murmuring in my ear, it all seemed suggestive and deliciously indelicate.

We parted sedately and businesslike at the end of the appointment—she with my dental insurance information, and I with a newly canalled tooth and the sweet whisperings of her intestines still ringing in my ears.

I have little knowledge of the courage of dentists, but I had one opportunity to experience it firsthand, and don't wish for further demonstrations. When our children were small and we lived in southern California, we used to camp in the San Bernardino Mountains. One weekend our site was next to a dentist and his young family. Dr. Petti was aloof and cool in his professionalism, especially when he heard that I worked in a book warehouse and was a poet, but his wife was gregarious. She invited us to play bridge with them that evening after supper.

We dealt cards at their picnic table by light of a Coleman lantern and the children played nearby. Dr. Petti ran his little troop with the authority of Toscanini. Suzanne and I had brought over a big box of Cracker Jacks as a treat for the kids, and he made a great show of not allowing *his* children to eat them. If they craved a snack he told them to eat an apple or banana.

Suddenly there was a great crash and thrashing in the darkness, we rose in alarm and gathered the children around us. Petti beamed his flashlight onto a very large brown bear absorbed in the contents of our garbage cans. Its massive head raised only momentarily to gaze at us before it continued ripping through the garbage bags, stuffing its mouth with half-eaten hot dogs, apple cores, and greasy potato chips.

Everyone scampered for the dentist's station wagon, children first, then the women. When they were all in, there was room for only one more. Dr. Petti did not for a moment hesitate to push himself in, taking the flashlight with him as he slammed the door, and then—believe me, please—looked out at me resolutely like a righteous executioner as he reached around and, one-by-one, pressed down the lock buttons on all the car doors, dismissing me to darkness and the great beast.

Indeed, it was more a job for a poet than a dentist. Poets have special discipline. They know how to pretend that they don't exist, how to freeze in place and hold their breath for a long time. I listened to the bear grind and snort through our leftovers, praying in a chill sweat that it would not seek to investigate further and come for the box of Goddamned Cracker Jacks I had left open on the picnic table.

When it was over and the bear went on to ravage other people's garbage, everyone climbed out of the car, sighing with relief and giggling nervously. Dr. Petti would not look at me. He snapped at his children, barking orders at them to prepare for bed. His wife seemed disconcerted and threatened. The evening was over. Only Suzanne came to comfort my shaking.

Next morning at dawn I awakened to hear Dr. Petti and his family quietly packing up their things. I thought about crawling out of my sleeping bag in my jockey shorts and making him say goodbye. Instead I listened to them drive away before I went back to sleep.

For a while when I was in my thirties, I had difficulty with my molars. A dentist suggested I have my wisdom teeth removed, but he indicated that there might be a problem. The roots of my wisdom teeth were curved slightly around nerves that might be injured in the extraction, causing my tongue and gums to go numb. Despite this highly undesirable possibility, the dentist pressed the issue and, sensing that I would not do it myself, had his assistant call and make an appointment with an oral surgeon named Clyde Berglars.

Dr. Berglars's technician assistant shot a series of x-rays. As she developed them, I could hear him banging around in another office and talking to an associate. Finally, when the x-rays were on the light table, he burst into the room, wearing a white rubber butcher's apron with a splash of blood on it. He looked like Vince Lombardi. He introduced himself, then patted me doughtily on the arm as he turned to study my x-rays, leaning over to get his big nose close to them.

I recalled how in Frank Norris's novel, *McTeague,* his brutish dentist character had "a head like that of a carnivora." The great ambition of his life was to have "a huge gilded tooth, a molar with enormous prongs" hung outside the window of his second floor office. His hands were like wooden mallets, and he often "dispensed with forceps and extracted a refractory tooth with his thumb and finger." Doc Holliday was a dentist, too, and a very rough character. Before he died of tuberculosis he killed many men in gun and knife fights, and shot it out with some fabled westerners at the O.K. Corral.

"Jesus Christ!" Berglars bellowed. I risk credibility by telling you that his colleague's name was Igor. But it was. "Igor," he called, "come in here." Igor looked like an undercard pug. "Take a look at *this!*" At that moment I decided never to return to this office. I even considered bolting right then as they pored manfully over my x-rays, but envisioned these two brutes running me down like linebackers and crippling me.

"We'll have to turn those suckers somehow as they're coming out," Berglars said to Igor as he poked his thick finger on the film. He turned to me and gripped my forearm. "Whadaya say, Paul? Let's make an appointment and get it done. I think we can pull it off. You might as well get it over with."

Sure. A numb mouth for the rest of my life—never to taste fresh tomatoes or pork chops or beer again. Baby lima beans or apples or trout. Pumpkin pie or chicken or Greek olives. Sure, get it over with. Suck it up! Strap it on!

I never saw Berglars again. His assistant called my office several times and left messages, but I did not even consider returning the calls. Later I compromised and had my left side wisdom teeth extracted by a less hectoring oral surgeon. He could not turn the teeth enough to avoid nerve damage. The left side of my tongue and gums remain numb, even after all the years—but I retain enough taste buds on the right to know the difference between *pâté de campagne* and peanut butter.

Suzanne and I were logy with jetlag. We drove the short distance from Puivert to Lavelanet in the late morning to buy basic groceries, forgetting that stores and services close for a two hour lunch in the south of France. So we wearily found a restaurant and ordered omelets, salads, and a demi-carafe of white wine. In France if you are stuck somewhere you can at least expect to buy a decent lunch. Under similar circumstances in America you are in for a bout with indigestion to go with your impatience.

There was nothing to do but take our time—the stores would not open again until two-thirty. Time enough for lunch *and* a nap—a very civilized custom. I sometimes wish I had lived my whole life in the south of France.

I chewed a piece of bread crust and was on my second mouthful of omelet when I bit something small and metallic. I spit it into my palm— one of my gold crowns nuzzled amongst egg fluff, bright in the sun streaming through the restaurant windows, cracked into two pieces.

I groaned and Suzanne looked up from her salad. I picked the pieces of gold out of the egg and showed them to her. "My God!" she said. "How did you do that?"

"I have a talent."

"What will we do now?"

"Find a dentist."

A day later, after halting consultation with our French neighbors in Puivert, we located Dr. Maurin's office in an ancient townhouse just off a medieval square in the nearby village of Chalabre. We were assured that he is a "bonne dentiste." We pushed open his heavy front door and entered a dingy hallway, looking for a reception desk. To the right was a waiting room where two elderly French women were seated on worn vinyl chairs. There were two wooden benches as well, one covered with a dirty orange cushion for seating, the other stacked with tattered French sporting magazines, most of them at least two years old.

We smiled nervously at the women, "Bonjour, mesdames," and sat down on the cushioned bench. Across the hall we could hear what was unmistakably a doctor and patient quietly talking. Ten minutes later the door opened; the patient departed. We were expecting an attendant, but Dr. Maurin walked into the waiting room, a thin, dark man with graying hair and brown, intelligent eyes. He nodded to the two women, then looked at us in puzzlement. It was time for Suzanne to trot out her halting French. A "nomination." We wished to have a "nomination." Her "mari" had cracked a "dent."

"Anglais?" he asked. He shook my hand, then Suzanne's.

"Non. Américain."

"Ah," he said.

I don't know what he was thinking. The French semiologist, Jean Baudrillard—a bit of a smart aleck—said, "Americans may have no identity, but they do have wonderful teeth."

Dr. Maurin motioned for us to follow him into his office. The mesdames looked piqued. I was the last one out of the room. I smiled awkwardly, gave them my best Old World bow and said, "Pardone-mwah." They looked at each other.

Dr. Maurin's office was a large room on the street side of the house, painted in an unobtrusive dirty cream color. His dental chair was mounted near the heavily draped front window. There were cabinets built in along the wall. At the other end of the room was a large antique table, piled with papers and forms.

I had wrapped my broken gold cap in a paper napkin and put it in my wallet. I took it out to show him.

"Ah," he said. I would need a new "capuchon." How long would we be in France?

"Six semaines." Could something "temporaire" be done?

"Non, non." Here he launched into an extended explanation in French, of which we understood not a single syllable, but obviously indicating that I would have to run the whole course—x-rays, impressions, and a new crown built. We determined this through much pawing of pocket dictionaries, pointing, and gesticulating. Suzanne had a French phrase book, which included examples of French sentences that might be useful in a dental office. Dr. Maurin was much interested in this, seemed almost grateful for it, pointing out passages that described my situation. Fortunately he had a sense of humor. He concluded by saying that, yes, we would need to make some "nominations." Did we have "assurance"?

American insurance, we said. We would pay him ourselves and turn it into the American company when we got home. We expected then to be shown to a secretary, but he uncovered a dog-eared appointment book, shuffled more papers until he found a pencil, and we agreed on two nominations which he scrawled into his diary.

I did not want to have a new French cap for my tooth. I wanted him to just cement a slug onto the remains of my tooth until I could see my dentiste Américain. I did not want to come back to that dismal office and have Dr. Maurin poking around in my mouth with sharp, dirty instruments.

On the airplane I had been reading J. K. Huysman's novel, *Against Nature*. The abysmal, jaded hero develops a toothache and requires an extraction. Because he is in abject pain, but sated and bored with life, desiring new experiences, he subjects himself to a cheap dental quack in the bowels of Paris. The wooden steps leading to the extractor's second floor office are soaked with blood. The dentiste-boucher takes hold of the tooth with a huge pair of pliers, puts his feet against the chair arms and practically lifts the hero out as the extraction is made, then hands him a big, stained bowl to bleed into.

I was still suffering from the distortions of jetlag. I was a disoriented stranger and could only speak the language like a one-year-old. How would I communicate with Dr. Maurin? Did he understand what "ouch" meant? I looked around for traces of blood. The office was shadowy and threatening in the afternoon light, perhaps there were air hammers or crowbars or fire tongs stored in the cabinets.

Dr. Maurin escorted us to his office door and shook hands. He seemed quite pleasant, but he looked a bit like photographs I have seen of the demented Paul Verlaine. The mesdames looked at us testily as we passed the waiting room on our way out.

A week later we returned to Dr. Maurin's office. What looked like the same two French women were seated in his waiting room. "Bonjour, mesdames." When Dr. Maurin looked into the room he seemed surprised and a little miffed when he saw us. He spoke to us in French. "We got the nomination wrong," Suzanne said. "We were supposed to be here yesterday." We were mortified. The mesdames were appalled. Dr. Maurin was very kind, motioned for us to follow him into his office. I bowed awkwardly again to the ladies as we left the room and they were incredulous.

We attempted to express our shame. I offered to pay him. He waved my money away and found his dilapidated appointment book amongst the rubble on his desk. "Mercredi, à deux heures de l'après-midi." He wrote it out on a scrap of paper for us. Then he wrote it in English, "Wednesday, two o'clock, afternoon."

As we were leaving, the hemp mat caught under the massive door as we tried to heave it shut. Dr. Maurin had already taken one of the women into his office, but the other sat watching us disdainfully as we struggled to free the heavy door. I attempted to force it, but the mat only wedged in tighter and the rug crumpled beneath it, jamming the door even more. "You'll have to pull it out," Suzanne said.

I got down on my hands and knees and began tugging on the mat as Suzanne pushed on the door. Every citizen of Chalabre and surrounding towns had wiped their feet on that mat and it was filthy. Finally we managed to dislodge the door and it banged against the wall resoundingly amidst a great puff of dirt. The madame looked away in disgust. Dr. Maurin came to his office door and peered out. We smiled and waved, bowing our ways out.

If I crack my crown in Soldiers Grove, Wisconsin, I call Dr. Tribby's office in Boscobel. One of the three receptionists answers the phone. I first give her my name and she brings my records up on her computer screen. What is the problem? When I respond, she asks if I am having pain. When I say no she gives me an appointment three weeks hence and asks for my dental insurance information. She gives this to the insurance accountant for recording. She assures me that they will call the day before to remind me of my coming appointment.

I spend three weeks tonguing the gap in my molars and gingerly chewing on the opposite side. I receive the reminder call the morning before my appointment day, and when I arrive at the office I check in with one of the three receptionists and she gives give me a form to fill out. An assistant comes out to fetch me and I am escorted to one of three brightly lit treatment rooms where I am aproned with a fresh, sterilized cloth and laid back gently in the chair. She probes my tooth base and asks me questions, then places a heavy lead blanket across my chest and takes some x-rays. I can hear Dr. Tribby in another treatment room talking to a patient.

When the x-rays are developed, he comes in looking like a spaceman, a breathing mask over his mouth, a white surgical cap, and a plastic shield covering his face. He washes his hands and slips on a pair of thin, white, rubber gloves out of a sterilized package. He uses my first name. He asks if I want Novocain. I ask if there will be much pain. He says, "I don't think so, Paul—but it won't hurt *me*." I choose numbness. He studies the x-rays on the light tray. As he probes my tooth root he is very chatty and friendly. The assistant stands by his side and he talks to her as she makes notes on my record. He looks at the x-rays, then brings around a small water jet and washes out my gap. The assistant puts a hissing suction tube in my mouth, tells me to close my lips, and the wash water is sucked from my mouth. All the instruments and equipment are kept out of my sight until they are used. Dr. Tribby brings around a high speed drill with a grinder and works at my gap. My mouth is sprayed again and sucked dry.

The clay has already been prepared and mounded on the u-shaped plate by another assistant. By the time the impression has been made, the first assistant has prepared cement and a small disc. She hands Dr. Tribby a pair of small forceps and he glues the disc into place in my gap, pats my shoulder, and heads for another patient. A timer has been set and when it rings, an assistant squirts out my mouth again and sucks it dry. My apron is removed and I am escorted back to the waiting room. The assistant hands my records to one of the receptionists and I make another appointment.

In two weeks the routine is much the same, except there is now a trainee on hand, so now there are three assistants parading in the room as Dr. Tribby fits in my new gold cap. It takes some adjustment and grinding to make the fit right. On my way out the receptionist asks for my insurance card again, then points out that it has been more than six months since I have had my teeth cleaned. So I make another appointment.

When we came to Dr. Maurin's office again we found that he worked entirely by himself, not a clerk or assistant in sight. He displayed extraordinary good cheer with my inability to understand even his simple requests to open or close my mouth. He expertly shot his own x-rays, spooned clay from a can into the u-shaped holder as I watched, made the impression, then affixed a temporary cap, all the while asking me to do my own mouth washing and spitting from a paper cup that he filled with water at the press of a button.

His small children played in the hall outside his office as he worked on me. At one point they called to him. "Papa! Papa, ça va. Ça va!" He excused himself, took off his light blue dentiste jacket, and went off to silence them, then returned, put on his jacket again, and continued his work.

He asked me what my profession was. I flipped hastily through my pocket dictionary and tried to tell him that I am a retired publisher and a poet, but managed to say only in mangled French, as I realized later, that I am a retarded poet. He politely did not laugh. "Ah, a poète!" He was clearly impressed, his brown eyes sharp in the light from the half-shuttered window. "Quel distingué!"

Suzanne sat in the room with us to aid with communications. Her French is at best serviceable. Dr. Maurin talked on and on in French. Afterward she helped me to reconstruct just a little of what he said then: "As with painters, there are great neglected poets from the south of France. Do you know the poetry of Charlés Cros? An amazing artist, and beyond this, an inventor! Then there is the work of Frédéric Mistral? Ah, so beautiful! A Nobel winner. Then there was Paul Claudel and Paul Valery, who were also born in the south."

He went on and on passionately. We lost track of all that he said. Surely he realized this, but he was excited, and went on in rapid French. He was happy to have a patient he could say these things to. We were grateful for each other. He quoted verse. It did not seem to matter that I understood nothing. In fact, I *did* understand. For God's sake, he was reciting *poetry*—not scolding me for failing to floss twice a day, nor claiming that my molars and canines were the spiritual center of my life.

What had I been expecting from dentists? Certainly I had not been looking to feel at home with them. I was caught unawares. I had survived Doc Rubright, Clyde Berglars, Dr. Petti, and Victoria Plum to find, after almost a whole lifetime, Dr. Maurin, five thousand miles from home in the village of Chalabre, France.

During my third nomination Dr. Maurin set a beautiful silver metal molar in my mouth, fitting it perfectly on the first try. Now it glitters like a warm jewel amongst my gold ones—a special memory, like the little paperback edition of Charlés Cros's poems that he gave me. When he finished we stepped to his cluttered desk again. He found a pencil and wrote out a detailed bill for thirteen hundred francs, approximately two hundred dollars, never having asked for a deposit, although he did not even know my address in Puivert.

I would have given him a thousand bucks. I did not want to leave. Quietly I wondered if he had small rooms in the upper chambers of his large, ancient house which we might rent so we could spend our days listening to his drill, his sweet voice reciting, the small noises of his children playing outside his office. It was late, but not too late.

But Dr. Maurin walked us to his massive front door, carefully opened it himself, looked into our eyes, shook both our hands and smiled, then gently closed it after us.

My Afternoon with Duke

The heat was staggering on the cement and asphalt of Disneyland in the late afternoon sun. I had forgotten to put on sun lotion and my bare arms and forehead were parboiling. I wandered peevishly amidst the precious make-believe.

It was the early 1960s, I worked for a book distributor that serviced the park bookstore, and the Disneyland store manager had given me a free pass. Having nothing more exciting to do one day, I braved the Los Angeles freeways from Pasadena to Anaheim.

Forty years ago the park still smelled a little of fresh paint, and the fuzzy, costumed characters had genuine enthusiasm. But I was a young wag with a bad attitude. When Donald Duck came up to shake my hand, gargling and squawking, I sneered at him and walked away. I felt like the Marquis de Sade visiting kindergarten. Snow White, looking like a Danish sorority girl, was standing on a corner greeting people and giving directions as they passed by. I asked her if I could buy her a drink at the nearest bar.

I thought she might get a giggle out of this, but she played it straight. "I'm sorry, sir. Alcohol is not served in the park." She must have squealed on me, because later I noticed a park policeman looking me over. I shambled around irritably and was just starting to consider the cocktail hour in Anaheim, when from some distant corner of the park I heard a jazz piano noodling at a familiar tune. I recognized it as the introduction to "All Too Soon," an aberration in the midst of all the furry hand-wagging, super rides, and fake neighborhoods. I cocked my ear and was certain I heard Lawrence Brown tonguing and lilting the tune on his trombone, with saxophones riffing elegantly behind him. Unmistakably it was the Ellington orchestra.

I was aroused by the music and looked around at the passing crowd for kindred spirits. No one else paid the slightest attention. They were busy bustling around and shelling out hard money for their fata morgana. I wondered if the music was recorded; but the sound was too full, too thoughtful and imperfect to be recorded music.

I didn't want to run because of the policeman nearby, so I started shuffling swiftly along the walkways in the direction of the sound. The trombone was caressing the tune now, moving it around; then Ellington gave another flurry on the piano and the saxophones hit it hard behind him, pushing Brown to more choruses. They were working their way toward the conclusion, the trombone finishing the line of the song in front of the whole band now. I was scurrying, my excitement mounting as I tried to find the source. Just as I turned a corner beside a chain link fence, Ellington put a period at the end of the tune with his piano. I hurried past some hedges and there below me on a bandstand in a far corner of Disneyland was an improbable vision—the Duke Ellington Orchestra.

I cannot imagine anything more incongruous. It was as if W. B. Yeats had been invited to read at Woodstock, or Ingres admitted to a Dadaist exhibition. Outside the fence Mickey Mouse was waving and being cute, Goofy was scratching himself, the little bell on the Jungle River Ride boat was tinkling, the Matterhorn sleds were clattering in the distance, and here was the greatest illusion of all: In all its sophistication and erotic magnificence—the most famous jazz orchestra of all time, in gray jackets and dark blue pants, playing to an empty house in Disneyland.

The 1960s were the Elvis Presley–Chuck Berry Years—not a good time for jazz. The Beatles were about to record "I Want to Hold Your Hand." Many jazz musicians were heading out to Europe. You had to look hard to find jazz recordings in stores. Later I learned that, at this time, Ellington was working on some movie scores, including the award winning music for "Anatomy of a Murder," so probably the band was playing a few Los Angeles gigs. But *Disneyland?* Perhaps one of the board of directors was hip. Maybe the band was there to provide "color."

It was a gig in an unlikely time and place. I was transported, but no one else showed the slightest curiosity. The gate was open and there was no admission charge. In the midst of flabby, expensive make-believe, the band was staying busy. They were playing only for *me*—and I had walked in free. It seemed like some mistake.

But I sat down and listened in solitary grandeur. Between numbers I slipped down to the front row and sat right under Duke's piano so I could see his face. He did not look at me. He was brooding and seemed bored, a man doing some workaday work without much enthusiasm and no hint, at least that day, of any real possibilities. If I had been part of a crowd of thousands, I would have meant no more or less. As it was, I seemed almost an irritant. Though I was stirred and demonstrative, there wasn't enough of me.

I got close-up views of the soloists as they stood to play—the somber, baggy-eyed Johnny Hodges, Ray Nance with a little mud on his shoes, Cootie Williams, the muscular Cat Anderson, and the authoritative Harry Carney. It was a miracle. They were mine alone to dig. But the musicians were not smiling either, and they were not playing for me—they were playing for themselves.

Ellington stayed hunched over the piano keys, wearing a magnificent crimson velvet jacket and gray slacks. Of course, he looked terrific, but he never stood to show me the full Ellington splendor. He announced the numbers perfunctorily, bent over his piano mike, and he never looked in my direction.

It was molten as the afternoon sun descended. At one point, between numbers, Hodges stood to take off his band jacket and drape it over the back of his seat. It seemed almost an act of defiance. Sam Woodyard, the drummer, Peck Morrison, the bassist, and several others gratefully followed suite. Duke had his head down and paid no attention. He kept his velvet jacket on and his face was glazed.

They sauntered through "Mood Indigo," "Summertime," "Do Nothing Till You Hear from Me." Still no other person came into the seats, but I continued to give them my singular enthusiasm. Then with the toy Disneyland train tweeting like a silly canary in the distance, Ellington announced with some emphasis, as if he was finally gathering his strength, that they were going to play "Happy Go Lucky Local."

He started the engine by swinging some train sounds on his keys, with Woodyard rolling his snares behind him. The saxophones and trumpets started moving down the track, making the whistle blow, then soloists took turns, as if they were looking out at the passing scenery—Jimmy Hamilton, Carney, Hodges, Russell Procope, taking sweet looks out the windows, with Cat Anderson screeching the engine around the big curves. Ellington was setting the course, growling at the keys. He soloed again with great energy. They were all busy now, astir, doing some good work, happy to be really swinging at last for each other. The saxophones rolled the long train over the ties; the trombones bounced it along as the trumpets worked the whistle. They were having fun.

Paul Gonsalves, the irrepressible Mexican Bandit, stood to take a buoyant solo, pulling the cars through some very groovy scenery. A few of the musicians clapped rhythmic encouragement for him. Ellington was down on the keys pushing Gonsalves with subtle, little supports. The whole band bounced it again behind him, howling the whistle, making cut time, headway time, then finally easing it in, closing the number with Cat Anderson shrieking it to a triumphant stop at the station.

I stood to pound my little paws together until they were pink. At last Duke had a trace of a smile. Still he did not look at me. He didn't have to. After all the years, he knew who I was. I mattered a little, but then I did not matter at all. There was only one of me that day—and I had gotten in free. But by God, I was *there*, and so they had given me a little gift.

Duke stood up from the piano and the rest of the musicians started shuffling offstage, lighting cigarettes and talking quietly to each other. He came at last to the stage mike. His eyes flickered over me momentarily; then he looked off across the empty seats. He seemed weary, but he thanked me for attending and said he wanted me to know that I was very beautiful, very sweet, very gracious, very generous, and that he loved me madly.

Part Three ∽

And in his brain,
Which is dry as the remainder biscuit
After a voyage, he hath strange places crammed
With observation, the which he vents
In mangled forms.
  —William Shakespeare, *As You Like It*

Small Places

Shed, hut, hovel, shack, shelter, sheepfold, henhouse, cabana, hutch, isba, coop, cottage, cot, cote, lean-to, shanty—whatever they are called, there seems to be one tenet for their construction—an ancient custom springing from necessity or perhaps secret longing. Even if intended essentially for storage, they are at least built long enough one way so that a person can lie down to rest, live, hide, or escape in them. They can be welcoming when we are astray, warm as the never forgotten womb.

I am always fascinated by small places when I come across them in the countryside or back alleys of towns. After some years of living in endlessly urban Los Angeles, late one autumn I flew home to Ohio to visit my ailing parents. My father met me at the airport wearing his overcoat, fedora, and scarf. I had been living in California for almost seven years and my mind was on my mother's illness. I had forgotten to bring a coat and shivered as I walked with him through the parking lot.

But on the drive home I was exhilarated by bright foliage and warmed by the sight of old farms set in the trees and fence lines. Nothing was old in Los Angeles, so the sight of barns and especially venerable sheds transported me. They were symbols of a faraway place and time I had forgotten. They seemed foremost of all the things I had missed about the rooted landscape and pronounced seasons of the Midwest. Memories flowed as my father drove me through the radiant countryside.

I had not lived on a farm as a child, but we visited the farms of friends and relatives. I had never helped to build a shed or tear one down, but they seem so requisite to the countryside, quietly waiting and serving; places not often used but very necessary, they stand undisturbed for weeks and months until someone opens them and surprises their abiding darkness. The door shrieks on its hinges, things scurry into the shadows as the walls crack and gasp with surprise. You do not tarry when you enter, you quickly take what you need—a tool, bag of seed or fertilizer—then you shut the door and move on with your work. If someone spends a lot of time hanging around inside sheds, they probably are adrift, in desperate need of rest or escape, or perhaps they are up to no good.

My childhood friend Marty Folsom and I came across some guys in a small place who were up to no particular goodness. Folsom's family always wanted to live "in the country" and eventually moved from our city neighborhood to an old farmhouse on a forty-acre plot outside of Canton. I loved to visit them. The Folsom acres seemed very rural to me and Marty enjoyed showing off his fields and woods.

He was a frail, articulate kid, a prolific story-weaver and white liar, my most imaginative friend. He had a pale, triangular face and dark hair, walked like a bird with a kind of bounce off the balls of his feet, flapping his hands loosely on his wrists as if he was about to take flight.

His mother indulged him in his most extravagant stories and schemes, but his father irritably corrected him and punished him when he went too far astray. I knew Marty was not "lying." He was just improving reality. He believed everything he said and was hurt and surprised when he was harshly corrected. Eventually we went our own ways and fell out of touch. Years later I was stricken to read in the newspaper that he committed suicide in his early twenties, apparently never having felt comfortable with unimproved reality.

We made up wonderful games to play when I visited the farm and exhausted ourselves prowling the acreage. The fields were rented out for haying by the Folsoms, and we followed the mowers and rakes, pretending we were outraged Indians bewildered by civilization.

Along a fence surrounded by brush there was a sagging, abandoned shed and we used it as one of our hideouts. It was built low and had been used for tools and equipment storage, but now it was badly weathered. We were surprised one chilly Saturday morning to find the shed door open and two hay field workers lounging on the floorboards, eating their lunch and paging through jungle comic books. They were grubby guys wolfing down Bond Bread balogna sandwiches and swigging quarts of cherry pop. One of them was big, hairless, dressed in bib overalls and a stained work shirt; the other was smaller and darker with a ragged moustache and hair growing out of his ears, his glasses cloudy with field dust. Both of them smacked their lips as they chewed. The men looked at guileless, loquacious Marty with disdain, but Marty was oblivious as he jabbered at them, carefully pronouncing his words and gesturing dramatically. Finally the filthy little man interrupted the monologue and spelled out, "F-u-c-k." I took Marty's elbow and tried to move him toward the door.

"Do you know what that spells, smart boy?" the man asked. Marty faltered, then went on talking as if the man had not spoken.

The man put down his pop bottle, leaned toward Marty and made a lewd suggestion. Marty stopped talking. Finally he said, "Does my dad know you guys are in here? You better get out."

The man laughed and rolled his scurrilous eyes at the cobwebs and insect nests on the ceiling. "Kid, nobody owns the inside of this shed."

I grabbed Marty firmly now and pulled him out the door. He was uncharacteristically silent as we walked through the stubble back to his house. Our field games were over. We felt numb. Marty was thinking hard. Finally, plainly bewildered, he asked, "What was he talking about? Should I tell my dad?"

"I don't know, Marty. Let's go play a game of Monopoly," I suggested.

Many years later I finally found my very own shed in northwestern Pennsylvania. I was not lost, desperate, or up to no good—I was just hiding. We moved to Pittsburgh in the late 1960s and scraped up enough money to buy a weekend cabin in the woods and fields near Clarion. We were an active, vociferous family and the cabin was small. I needed a quiet place to work on poems, so I took over a small shed set away from the house. I tacked up insulation and cheap paneling, sawed squares out of the walls, and fitted in two old windows I found at the dump. I cut a piece of plywood for a desk and set it up on a two-by-four frame, put in a folding chair, and began arising early on weekend mornings to work on my writing.

It was a wonderful adventure, the first time in my life that I actually inhabited a small place. It came to be almost a living presence for me. I sensed it becoming accustomed to my weekend intrusions, and I grew to be part of its existence along with rabbits and woodchucks that burrowed under it, spiders that softened its corners with their webs, and flies that mobbed the glass at the change of seasons. Hornets and wasps nested and guarded the eaves outside. We all worked hard together. I listened to the shed standing against the wind, watched through my windows as snow flittered down, and cherished the soft paradiddle of rain on its roof.

I wired it and brought in an electric heater. In winter I trudged out through drifts and yanked the frozen door open, clapped my hands and danced until the heater had worked for a while. I took up the life of this small place and it was good for me and for my poems.

In old times small places were flimsy structures—roofs on poles or lean-tos to provide some dryness or shade. Eventually the sides that faced hard weather were enclosed. Sometimes they were attached to houses or barns, but mostly they were built freestanding and completely enclosed in the middle of fields, along fences, in back alleys of towns, or near gardens.

People adrift sometimes use them in passage. Over years they are challenged by the elements. It is expected that eventually they will wear out and fall apart. Now they can be replaced easily with prepackaged structures that are assembled from printed directions and templates, bolted together, and shaped like old barns or cute gingerbread houses. It is no longer necessary to sink footers, build frames, drive nails, and smash one's thumb with a hammer.

The old wooden sheds are like extended memories. In some ways they define us. They stand and serve until mildew and dry rot overwhelm their shrinking boards, especially if they were built with inferior wood or if they are poorly located in boggy ground. The joints and corners grow spongy and the soft disease creeps up the fibers and gets under the tin roof. Termites or carpenter ants get into old, untreated wood, into the heart of the shed, and gnaw its strength, reducing its tension until it collapses into its own dust in the wind.

There are not many old wooden sheds in towns anymore, mostly just padlocked, precut, sheet metal dollhouses. I don't know where lost people hide these days. But I remember Leonard. I never knew his last name, never exchanged a manifest sound with him, nor did any of the other boys. He spoke a language that was distant and strange.

We would already be sitting in the bed of the truck with our mowing equipment when the driver picked up Leonard on a corner of 12th Street on the way to the parks. He climbed slowly over the tailgate as some of the boys heckled him and held their noses. He smiled, sat down, and began packing his cracked, taped-up pipe with tobacco, pretending he could not hear us. A soiled man, teeth rotten to the gums, with hair like gray, electric shock, he must have been almost sixty years old. We did not think much about that. Yes, he was old, but he talked funny and he was unwashed. He did not demand the respect we gave to most other older people. He did not have a wife or family or language we could understand. He was one of us, but set apart with a small group of oddballs who were tormented. It did not matter that he could outwork any of us—eight hours without a break on a jug of water and his sack of day old bread. He wasn't like other older men— our fathers and uncles.

Thank the Lord the park supervisors had the kindness to let him work alone. The truck dropped him off with pruners and a ripsaw at the biggest clumps of unkempt bushes in the park. By day's end when we picked him up, he would be sitting on the ground smoking his busted pipe, the bush subdued, trimmed to cane, tied in neat bundles ready for hauling. He pulled himself wearily over the tailgate and sat downwind from the teenage wisecracks. He was oblivious, indestructible, a prodigious worker. Secretly I thought he was amazing.

Usually I took the bus to my summer job with the parks, but one day I borrowed a friend's car and was driving home when I saw Leonard trudging down the street. I drove on by. I knew it was a low thing to do and felt awful. I stopped, backed up, and rolled down the car window.

"Can I give you a lift?"

Leonard was astonished. He looked at me uncertainly. I leaned over and pushed the car door open, gesturing toward the passenger seat. He tried to wave me on, shaking his head and smiling. I beckoned again more emphatically. He hesitated, but then got into the car. I indicated that he should point out the directions and he understood.

It was a long way through some patchy neighborhoods. We ended up driving beside an abandoned railroad track until we arrived at a small, deserted storage shed where Leonard stopped me. This was his home. He had mended it with old shingles and siding lugged in from dumps and painted it dark green.

He smiled his gratitude, climbed out of the car, but did not shut the door. Instead he beckoned that he wanted me to come into his home. I shook my head, trying to show that I had to hurry on, but he was persistent, held his thumb and forefinger up indicating something small. I assumed he meant he wanted me to step in just briefly to see his home, so reluctantly got out of the car.

I had to stoop as I entered. The shed was dark until he switched on a bare light bulb hung over a scuffed table and chair. I saw a cot against one wall. He'd hung some shelves where he kept a few chipped dishes, pans, and utensils; on a wider shelf at the bottom were a hot plate, some bottles, jugs of water, cans of baked beans and Spam. The place smelled of Leonard and stale tobacco smoke. There was a crucifix on the wall and two framed yellowed photographs—one of a pretty young woman, the other of an old couple, the man seated and the woman standing with her hand on his shoulder. They looked Old World and obscure like Leonard. A cracked, potbellied railroad stove stood in the corner. I had never been in such a small, lonely place as Leonard's home.

He shuffled around and pretended to do some tasks. I could tell he felt uneasy about his surroundings. He motioned that I should sit down in the chair, and, taking up one of his bottles from the shelf, he poured a few drops of amber liquid into a jelly jar and proudly set it in front of me. I was wary and uncertain, but he waited smiling until I took a taste.

I expected the worst, but it was delicious and magical. Thinking back and remembering that flavor on my young, untested palate, I believe it might have been a plum wine. Whatever it was, Leonard had made it, and it was the best thing he had to offer. It was gladsome and pleasantly warm even on that long ago summer day. I was not used to drinking alcohol. He knew this and gave me only a tiny bit. Just enough to let me feel his gratitude for bringing him home to his small place.

∾

I still study small places wherever I go and imagine their history. Centuries before prefabricated pole sheds and treated sheet metal New England and European farmers built enduring structures of fieldstones that now have become antiques; travel poster subjects in the fields of Maine or Connecticut, Provence or Scotland. I always stop the car and gaze at them. But it is opportunistic and ephemeral to exalt sheds. Like stones and trees they will outlast all efforts to present them as art. An exasperated British art critic wrote of a recent exhibition of "Y.B.A.'s" (young British artists), "The shed is Art now, you see, and if you don't understand why, that's because you are not clever or cool enough—a case of emperor's clothes if ever there was one."

Suzanne and I now live in the upper Midwest of America where early farm sheds were built plainly with plentiful hardwoods instead of stones and, like human beings, are "useful" only for some decades. Eventually time and hard weather wear them down and they become exhausted and abandoned. If they are not torn or burned down, they sag for many years, slumping like ghosts in foggy morning pastures, oblivious to their deterioration.

For a dozen years I watched from the window of my writing shack an abandoned Wisconsin shed, listening to it wail and strain on its rusty nails as it bore up under high winds and driven rain. When I took a break from words I often walked out with our dog to look at this derelict. I knew its warped, gray boards intimately, plumed with frost marks and long finger-shaped stains from melting ice and wet snow. When I stepped inside it was, I imagined, like being under an abandoned spider web or entering an old wasp nest—tattered but still resigned. It remained useful to many creatures. The light inside was constricted, smelling of mold and animal waste. The roof creaked and threatened to collapse on our heads and this made Sheba nervous.

We retreated to our writing shack to scribble and doze in the sweep of light and shadows. My knees grated under the desk as I gazed out at the shed and my spine ached dully as if pulling against flagging rafters. When the wind was high the dog and I did not go near the shed, but watched from the window as it listed and tottered, almost billowing in the currents.

One placid summer morning that was no different than any other quiet day, as subtle as a change of seasons, the shed collapsed. It went down on its own early, before we arrived on the scene. There must have been a tremendous clatter, but like Bishop Berkeley's tree, no one was there to hear it fall. After all the years of hanging together it became a pile of shivers in a matter of moments. I envision it suddenly listing and popping its clapboards, fanning them out and splintering into a heap, throwing up a dusty cloud into the unseen stars of the early morning sky.

It had not given in to the indignities of snow or blizzards, or high, impetuous winds under driven skies. It simply fell down on itself into the oblong of its foundation amidst weeds and saplings on one of the sweetest days of the year, providing me with a metaphor and example for the rest of my life.

I think about my own wooden writing shack where I sit now in Wisconsin. I had it built plain and apart beside a rise in the gravel road. Everyday I come to it and spend my hours with the words. Already a dozen years old, it begins to fray and tatter, and its windows rattle in hard weather. In fifty or more years, long after Sheba and I are gone, it will start to list and moan like a phantom.

I pray that it goes down on its own without witnesses, on a calm day not chosen by the wind, having done all it could do, quietly serving animals, insects, lost people, dogs, and poets who seek to rest, work, or escape.

Moon Talk

On nights when we were not going out for a bomb test and the moon was high over the Nevada desert, I borrowed Sergeant Easter's binoculars and walked down a dirt road away from the tent camp, to a big desert rock I had claimed for my nocturnal ramblings.

As I ambled in the moonlight I took off my fatigue cap and stuffed it into my pocket. My shadow slipped ahead of me on the road. I was uneasy alone in the desert night, but the unrelieved tedium of the drill in camp compelled me to challenge myself. I wanted to be by myself, away from the bravado and banter, and visit only with the silent moon.

Usually I carried a can of sardines and a package of crackers in my field jacket and toted a quart of beer from the Post Exchange. I climbed to the top of the rock and sat for hours, gazing and munching. I worked at some of my first poems in that reflected light, talking to myself and chewing on a pencil stub. Just a few miles away, over the next rise, was the blasted, pockmarked earth of the Atomic Energy Commission test site.

What did I think of, those nights, sitting on the rock in the pale light? I cannot remember. Romance certainly. Girls assuredly. Probably I fussed about the future. I must have spent time wondering about God; and then probably, under the broad sweep of those desert skies, I pondered the possibility of life on other planets. Mostly I just looked at the moon and wrote.

Sergeant Easter's field glasses were good; I was always astonished when the craters and dry ocean floors of the moon came vividly into focus. The great distance diminished and the proximity of that chalky circle made me feel tenuous as I gazed from the scourged landscape of the test site to that other one high in the sky.

My French grandfather once cautioned me when he found me moongazing. "Do not look at it too much," he said, "It can take you up." But I visited the moon those nights in Nevada. Callow and frightened by what we were doing in the desert, I cast myself up and took great comfort from it. For a few hours it made some sense of things as I worked at poems, and it helped me maintain my balance through appalling experiences.

I do not recall looking at the moon on bomb test nights, when we were ordered into trenches near ground zero to wait for the detonations. My mind was on other things then. Perhaps the AEC selected moonless nights so they could observe the full effect of their conflagrations. But in that dismal period of my life, down on my knees in the trenches of Hades, the desert moon was something I could count on, fickle in its movements, yet true, a figure of radiant comfort. I tried to put it into the poems I wrote and kept folded in the pocket of my fatigue shirt.

Eight years later I was still working at poetry, and the moon continued to rise and fall over my life and into my poems. A few of my pieces were published in magazines. I had become a bookseller in California. Suzanne and I had married, and we had an infant son.

One night Erik awakened, crying from a bad dream. Nothing would comfort him until I finally carried him out into the backyard. The moon was high and full, so I held him up to see it, a vision strong enough to settle him, and he quieted. "Moon!" I said. "Moon!" He was dazzled, struggled with the word until he croaked, "Moo, moo!"

Next day when I came home from work I went to his crib. He was playing with his toes, but looked up and brightened when he saw me. "Moo!" he said, the memory rising behind his eyes. "Moo!" It was our first secret together.

In a few years we moved to Pittsburgh and I worked for Pitt's scholarly press. In July of 1969 we were visiting my parents in Ohio when Neil Armstrong first put his boot-print in the moon's dust and declared it "a stark and strangely different place." My father, an old moon gazer himself, had gotten us all up in the middle of the night to see the television. He was enthralled as he held Erik on his lap, watching the astronaut's cautious movements in that strange light.

"Moo!" Erik said sleepily. He did not look at me. "Moo!"

"Why does he say that?" my father asked.

"It's a secret," I told him.

The astronauts looked like luminous turtles as they gingerly stepped on the white sands. They were cautious technicians. In the weeks before the landing, as I read newspaper accounts of Apollo's approach to the moon, I became troubled.

As a poet, I regarded the moon as my property. For eons it had been one of our most prominent, artistic images, the possession of composers, artists, night watchers, lovers, writers, dreamers, and children who need to be settled in the middle of the night. But it was falling into the hands of these scientific squatters, and now they were behaving rather familiarly with it. Neil Armstrong said, "It looks friendly to me." I took this bland pronouncement personally. I had been a moon watcher from childhood and now I felt voyeuristic, watching its purity besmirched.

I wanted to do something about this. I went home to Pittsburgh and, after weeks of rumination, decided I would gather an anthology of great writing about the moon. I had little time for this, with work, my own writing, and familial duties, but I was all energy in those salad days.

My only free time was my lunch hour, so each day at noon I took the elevator down from the 33rd floor of the Cathedral of Learning and, gnawing at my sandwich, quick-stepped across campus to the old Carnegie Public Library next to the museum. I gathered books from the open stacks, then hastened up the marble steps and plunked down in a chair in the reading room. The big, venerable tables smelled of vinegar and lemon oil as I put my nose down, and skimmed books for an hour. I copied out moon passages in long hand because the one primitive, copying machine cost a quarter a copy.

Early on I found a passage in Mark Twain that challenged me: "War talk by men who have been in a war is always interesting, whereas moon talk by a poet who has not been on the moon is likely to be dull." I knew Twain could be a wise guy and would say anything if he thought it might get a chuckle. But I was undaunted on those hard chairs, toiling in the reading room amongst Pittsburgh's nodding daytime scholars. Off campus there were people chatting in pleasant restaurants over quiche and a glass of wine, or wolfing down chilidogs at the Original Hot Dog—but day after day, at high noon I was collecting moon talk.

Amongst the votaries in the reading room, there was one man who claimed the same chair each day. He had a blunt nose, knobby gray skin, and looked like a Gila monster. If someone was sitting in his place, he stood staring at them, laden with books, until they gathered their papers and moved on. I imagined he must be working on an annotated edition of Schopenhauer or perhaps a history of the Children's Crusade, but I never got close enough to find out.

There were other, more congenial habitués working on projects in the room; a few of them nodded and smiled at me knowingly each day as I made my way in with my daily stack. We all had our secret tasks and whispered to each other only on rare occasions; but we were a pedantic force, quietly pulling for each other. I was the serial moon seeker.

I learned to scan books with great speed. The word "moon" is easy to spot in a text, and my eye became quick for it. My favorite quote was from an anonymous, 750-year-old poem, "Sir Patrick Spens." It seemed perfect to me and I doubt still that any moon talker will ever improve on it:

> Late, late yestreen I saw the new moone,
> Wi the auld moone in her arms.

This was better than the small talk of the astronauts. When Buzz Aldrin stepped on the moon a few minutes after Neil Armstrong, he declared it a "foreign situation with the stark nature of the light dark conditions." Hell, I knew this from just looking at it 250,000 miles away! In the reading room I found writers who had traveled to the moon and talked of it centuries before the astronauts walked on it. Their modes of travel were more ingenious than technical.

Listening to the drone of big floor fans in summer and radiators knocking in winter, I ferreted out the world's great moon writing. I was possessed, once again a captive of the moon.

Finally, I orchestrated a manuscript, typed it up, and began sending it to publishers. After two more years and twenty rejections, I abandoned the project. I figured I had given up five hundred lunch hours to it. That was enough, even for the moon; but it had been better than nibbling quiche or wolfing down hotdogs. Othello tries to explain his outré actions by saying:

> It is the very error of the moon.
> She comes more nearer earth than she was wont
> and makes men mad.

Even when I traveled over the years, I sought the moon. I recall riding a French excursion steam train at night, and the full moon angled and shifted through the coach windows as we turned the curves; it had followed us out of Chartres, flitting between trees and chimneys, slipping through plumes of engine smoke and thin curds of illuminated clouds. Now its light was glowing in the dewy fields and disappearing momentarily into patches of woods. Its reflection slipped over creeks and through cow ponds like a strong, luminous fish.

In the fields, French farmers had turned on their tractor headlights and were working in the dark. At first I wondered about this, then realized that they were planting by the full moon, as they have done for centuries.

Later I dozed in my seat, but the moon still tailed me, lifting the lids of my eyes, dipping into my naps, and gliding in and out of my fleeting dreams. I remembered my French grandfather's cautions about too much moon watching. The distant engine whistle seemed to resound from its craters. When we stepped out of the car at the end of the line, the inescapable moon was still with me.

On a camping trip, when my children were small, they decided to be brave and go night walking by themselves in the moonlit woods. They soon came barreling back into our campfire light. Something had been out there in the darkness, glowing and ugly.

I suggested that they might have disturbed a possum or raccoon. No, it was lit up like a ghost and shown through the trees. It was the moon. It had growled at them. "You *never* believe us!" they said.

But I did believe them. The moon can scare the snot out of you. When I was a grade school kid the movie, *The Wolf Man*, spooked me thoroughly, especially the scene when an appalled Larry Talbot staggers out of the woods after a night of carnage under the full moon. He steps into the firelight of the gypsy woman, and she tries to console him by eerily reciting:

> Even a man who is pure of heart
> and says his prayers by night,
> my son,
> may become a werewolf
> when the wolfbane blooms
> and the moon is full
> and bright.

That scene kept me indoors at night for a long time. When I was seeking moon talk in the library reading room I came across a rhyme in Mother Goose that I remembered from my childhood:

> The man in the moon looked
> out of the moon,
> looked out of the moon
> and said,
> "'Tis time for all children
> on the earth
> to think about going to bed!"

Yes, sir! And I kept my night light on all through my childhood.

After all the years, I remain respectful, still a seeker of moon talk. Somehow, by great good fortune, I have come to live in a perfect place for moon watching—on a cleared ridge top overlooking the woods and fields of a southwestern Wisconsin valley. Most nights I step outside to check the sky, trying to keep track of the moon in its slow, mysterious movements from full to gibbous to the delicate curl of its final phase.

The spring moon is all potential, a tight bulb of force, a light full of promise, a honeymoon, the most ultimate seed. The summer moon is proud, sweeping, pregnant, and content in its fecundity. Flattening as it rises out of the horizon, the autumn moon is brassy and ripe, boasting its triumph. The regal winter moon is often ringed by spectacular circles of ice crystals or is washed glowing through mackerel skies, but it seems cold and indifferent. Some winter nights the clouds are so thick the moon is not there at all, and, without the moon, the world becomes dismal as the inside of a crypt.

The five of us were sitting in the summer night by a bridge on a country road in Ohio, with the full moon rising over our heads. We had driven out far to escape the lights of Canton. The bridge was a good place to drink beer and talk quietly without disturbing anyone. We were jolly lads, liked to tease and push each other around a bit, but we were good friends and trusted one another.

It was late August and meteors were stroking the sky as we watched the full moon arc to the top of the night. Our talk was the light, occasional banter of young men. For no discernible reason a dog started howling from a farm in the distance. Another dog joined it from a different direction—then it was as if every dog in Stark County, distant and far, was barking and howling. They came on as though on cue from the moon, which seemed to be pulsating over our heads.

Austin lifted his head and began to ululate with them. We were surprised and amused, but it seemed a natural thing to do; so Beany hopped off the bridge railing and began to bell with Austin and the dogs. Soon Tucker took it up. Then Chase and I put down our cans and stood to join the chorus.

Yes, we were slightly loaded and loony, but this was more than just five young guys declaring their hormones—something else was happening. We joined the dogs in howl after howl, gulping to regain our breath, making waves of sound. The dogs responded, seeming to rejoice that we were joining them. Even if we had wanted to, we could not have stopped at that point. We looked at the moon and pumped our lungs, pursing our lips to focus our cries, cutting loose, our voices lifting higher and higher. It went on for minutes, and then we all stopped together, as if on some kind of notice; and the dogs were done, too, except for occasional yapping here and there.

We chuckled, all of us surprised and embarrassed by this spontaneity. But it had been impossible to resist, had felt necessary and good, almost celebratory—as if we had been thanking the moon for its fullness and expressing our gratitude for a period of time ending and a new beginning. The event was more terrestrial than cosmic, but we had reached out far enough beyond ourselves to touch the moon and proclaim this event.

It had been a common cry rising from dogs and young men. We felt refreshed, glad for the past, and anticipated the future, aware that a force not completely understood had held us. The moon put a spell on us, as it had on the dogs, and it called for our highest praise. There was no need for moon talk. We were quiet as we sat on the railing, subdued and humbled, sipping from our cans. Now the moon was on the wane, and, like the distant dogs, we rested together.

The Grass

Tread, cut, rip, cement, copy, burn, insult the grass; it returns and abides. You can destroy grass only by asking too much of it, then it deserts and leaves you with a sorry face of dust.

Slash of blades, teeth of animals, fire and water. It comes back. Fescue, rye, bamboo, clover, corn, reed, broom, bluestem, rice, cane, timothy, barley, wheat, foxtail, milo, flax, grain—just a small part of the list. Grass is indomitable, can grow over your head and make you disappear, can cover your house and swarm over your bed. It is your food and your poison.

Grass is green hindsight. Before I had memory, I know I tasted it. I placed my children in the grass when they were babes to learn its bitterness and sweetness. Like the sky, grass covers you when you die. Try to ignore it, but always it is under your feet, comes back through cracks in cement, out of ashes and dead earth, swarming over its own dead. It is triumphant in rain and sunlight, patient under snow and ice. Root, tuber, vein, blade, spike, node, sheath, floret, bundle, hollow stems, and joints where its leaves are attached. Over 635 genera, nine thousand species. Grass is long lists. It is more than the stars you can see in the sky. It is endless and despotic.

Mr. and Mrs. Triber owned a whole block in the middle of our neighborhood. In fact, it wasn't a block, but a large, triangle of grass between two odd-shaped blocks. In the center of the triangle, amongst trees, shrubs, and a massive landscaped lawn, stood their handsome, very upper-middle-class brick residence like a manor house in midst of our district's more modest frame houses.

Late every afternoon, I delivered their *Canton Repository*, placing it inside the door of their dimly lit, tiled entryway, and once a week I timorously pushed their doorbell, with my ring of punch card bills on my wrist to collect for the newspaper. Mr. Triber usually answered, and he was never happy to see me. None of my customers were. It meant they had to fumble around for their purses or change jars and come up with thirty-five cents as I waited at the door. Mr. Triber was aristocratic and aloof, but he seemed at least to be impressed by my doggedness.

Like most of my customers, the Tribers kept their bill card hung on a nail near the door. When they paid, I punched the week out of their card and the copy on my collection ring. Mr. Triber complained that the little circles of cardboard cluttered his entryway and were difficult to pick up, so he made me get down and pluck them up each week before I could go on my way.

My friend Carl Bartlow had the job of mowing the Tribers' grass. It was a big job, taking him many hours a week, but he was an assiduous boy, two years older than I, and he played flawless second base for the high school baseball team. I looked up to him, admired his moxie and industry. Bartlow got a job in a grocery store in the spring, and I was surprised when Mr. Triber asked if I would like to take over the lawn-mowing job. He showed me the shed where the equipment was stored and said, "You probably want to think about it. We expect a good job. Let me know in a couple of days."

Twenty-five bucks a month. That was a lot of lettuce in 1948. Added to my paper route money it meant affluence: jazz records, chocolate malts, baseball bats, bags of cashews, comic books, mad money to spend on girls. I was flattered that Mr. Triber thought of me as Bartlow's replacement, and I wasn't thinking clearly when I accepted his offer.

After this, grass loomed large in my life. The Triber lawn was extensive, sweeping from the point of their triangle, around each side of the house, and out through stands of large trees to the other two far corners. There were many landscaped banks and nooks to mow. Riding lawn mowers were not common in the nineteen forties. Mr. Triber didn't even have a gas-powered walking mower, but he was very proud of the heavy electric mower in his shed. He liked it because it was quiet and didn't disturb the tranquility of his green triangle. Reels of heavy black electric cord were stacked against the wall. Unrolled and plugged together they reached to all distant corners of the lawn.

Since I had to deliver newspapers in the afternoons and make collections for my route at least one night each week—plus mow our own lawn and do schoolwork—I had to schedule the Triber job for weekends. The trouble was, in my lust for money, I forgot that I was a fourteen-year-old kid who still liked to play and hang around with my buddies on weekends.

The first Saturday morning set the pattern. Mr. Triber gave me a key to the shed and I arrived shortly after breakfast, hauled out the big mower and spools. I started with the easy part, the open lawn running from the house out to the point of the triangle. Back and forth, forth and back—the pace of the mower was dead slow and the speed was not adjustable. But the cut grass smelled good and it was a lovely Saturday morning. It reminded me that my pals were down in the park hitting baseballs around.

Mr. Triber had warned me about running over the cord with the mower. It was a hazard. He showed me how to splice it if I had an accident. I tried to be careful as I played out line from the spool. After each row with the mower I had to stop and flop the cord to the side to keep it out of the way. It was stultifying work. The grass was boundless and absolute. After twenty or so turns with the mower I was lulled to inattention.

Two girls in shorts rode by magnificently on their bicycles, and I ran over the cord, severing it completely. I shut the mower switch off, unplugged the electric line, went to the shed for the pliers, insulation skinner, and black electrical tape. It took me twenty minutes to make a sloppy splice. This would not have been so bad, but I kept doing it, mangling the cord as I horsed the big mower around for another swipe. It began to look like a snake that someone had hacked with a hoe. By noon I had finished only half the section of open lawn and was bored to weariness. I had expected to finish the whole job by lunchtime. The afternoon dragged on and on. That first day was the beginning of the end. The grass had me down already.

I began to avoid the job, pretending that it didn't exist. Mr. Triber called and complained. His lawn grew shabbier and he more irritated and demanding. One Saturday morning I dragged myself to their tri-angle to work and found that the lawn had already been perfectly mowed and manicured. I rang the doorbell and Mr. Triber answered. He informed me, in grand, emphatic terms, that I no longer had the job. I was to turn in the shed key. "You are," he said, "in fact, fired." He had wooed Bartlow away from the grocery store and doubled his pay.

I had been defeated by the grass. Beyond the paper route, this was my first real job—and I had blown it. It was a hell of a beginning. I worried about the future, wondering how I would function in the adult world.

But the very next thing that happened pushed me back onto the grass. Before I could get the green smell out of my nostrils, my uncle got me a summer job mowing grass for the Canton Park Department. It seemed like penance—work was grass, grass was work, work was misery, mis-ery was grass, grass was adulthood, adulthood was work, work was mis-ery, misery was grass.

I toiled with a crew, trimming oval patches of grass around tree trunks that the rolling tractor mowers could not reach. I drudged with a hand mower and sickle, moving from tree to tree as the men roared back and forth on their tractors. The trees were endless. I looked for-ward only to lunch and break time. We lounged in the grass and the talk was of booze, sex, combat, and sports. I had little to contribute and, in any event, was generally too tired to participate.

Even the coming of the dreaded school year seemed like relief. But the following spring my uncle proudly announced that he had used his connections again to get me the summer mowing job again. There was no escape.

This time I was assigned to a sickle crew made up mostly of high school athletes staying in shape over the summer. I was the bottom of that pecking order and kept a low profile. We lined up like a chain gang along banks of cheat and brome and whacked at the grass all day in the full sun. The first boy to drop out spent the rest of the day in disgrace. Sometimes it wasn't me. For three sudoriferous months the grass grew and we cut it again. Then it grew some more, and we cut it again.

∾

When I was in basic training at Fort Knox, drill sergeant Moulds hated the sight of me and made me one of his personal harassment projects. It was his work to be abrasive, but I never understood his particular contempt for me. I took to the drill well enough, gave him no sass, held my eyes steady in formation, and shot straight with my weapons, but as far as Moulds was concerned, there was no possibility that I would ever do anything right. All he had to do was see me and his bulbous face turned into a bowl of cherry jello.

"Front leaning rest, motherfucker! Gimme ten."

Down on the grass I went to pump off ten pushups, struggling always with the last two or three, then leapt back up to attention.

"Looka those boots," Moulds bit the air. "What'd you do? Wipe your ass with them? Get 'em shined, you hear?"

"Yes, Sergeant Moulds."

He came up close and blew his wretched whiskey-coffee breath in my face. "Don't call me by my name, you sack of shit. Don't get familiar! You understand?"

"Yes, Sergeant!" This was not just normal drill sergeant ragging. He made a special point of detesting me. He gave the others plenty of heat, but he blistered me.

He enjoyed telling us we were professional killers. He particularly relished the way it shocked me. Basic training is done on the grass, four months of endless marches, rifle ranges, infiltration courses, hand grenades, machine guns, rocket launchers, bazookas, mortars, bayonet fighting. Sergeant Moulds stayed in my face through all of it.

We were on maneuvers, playing war games when I killed him in the grass. Our patrol was sneaking up on an enemy encampment when I raised my head and, peering through the tufts, saw Moulds standing just ahead with some cadre, poring over a map. I slipped my M-1 rifle into place. I had a full clip of blanks in my chamber and there was Moulds's face, red as an infected kidney, resting on top of my gun sight. We were to wait for a signal from our patrol leader to open fire, but I could not wait. I began pulling my trigger, squeezing off shot after shot. The others held their fire, but I emptied my whole clip. Moulds dropped to the grass and rolled, but I held him in my sights.

In the silence after this fusillade, he jumped up to see who had killed him. When he saw me, his big ears fell back and his jaw dropped like a backhoe. Like everywhere else—especially in the army—when you are dead, you are dead. I had disobeyed orders by firing without command, but he could not reprehend me. He was dead. His ass was grass.

Over the years my relationship with the grass has grown more subdued and reflective. When Suzanne and I lived in Iowa, we were in the middle of the tallgrass prairie, but there wasn't a blade in sight. The fields of corn and soybeans are planted right up to the foundations of farm buildings. Small patches of grass are mowed and trimmed around the houses, but the bluestem and Indian grasses that once grew higher than a man's head are long gone.

The first settlers claimed that the boundless fields of grass made them feel lonely. Beyond this, progress was to be made. The tallgrass was attacked and subdued. The plains of rich, black earth, created by centuries of rotting grass roots, were ploughed and planted with grains. At least half the United States is still covered with some kind of grass. The rest is sand, rock, asphalt, cement, beleaguered woods, and forest.

Suzanne and I live now amidst fields of grass and wooded slopes. For a while we rented our fields to a neighbor and he cut the hay, raked it, and hauled it away in huge bales. A few years ago we registered our fields with the Department of Natural Resources and set them aside for a decade of renewal.

Now our grasses grow high in the summers and I mow paths around the fields so we can take walks. I like the grass growing tall. It flowers and is alive with crickets, toads, bees, lightning bugs, birds, butterflies, and, yes, ticks and mosquitoes.

At times I feel uneasy, allowing the grass to grow. My instincts are learned and my lessons came hard. Grass is for cutting. Bend and swipe, bend and swipe, the blade ringing as I swing, whole vast fields and banks of grass. One boot planted slightly in front of the other, my T-shirt soaked, my head overheated and empty, I stop only to sharpen my blade, then onward, row after row—the American boy, the American man, swinging, cutting, shuffling on, rendering lines of grass, lines of words, leaving them straight behind. Dogged, inspired or uninspired, but work, work to be done, and work left behind. Even as I cut it, the grass is growing. The only thing left to do is finish, turn, and begin again.

The Road

Probably, if I had been consulted, I would have called it something corny like Bobolink Drive or Lark Rise Way or Turkey Trot. At the very least I would have prosaically called it Zimmerhill Lane. But a few years ago the post office decided to dispense with postal route and box numbers; so our township in southwestern Wisconsin put up a sign on our gravel road calling it Hutschenreuter Drive, after one of the early residents. Well . . . all right.

But now when I give out our address, I must brace myself for the repetitions and misspellings. "That's Hutschenreuter Drive. Yes, Hut-schenreuter. H-u-t-s-c-h-e-n-r-e-u-t-e-r." It is not a name that evokes birds to rise joyously from the meadows. But still, by any name, it is a handsome thing, our road, which takes a dogleg turn from the county highway, rounding for half a mile past two farms before it begins curving for a mile and a half on the weathered ridge top, turning what William Hogarth called "lines of grace and beauty," until it reaches our house.

It is a gravel road, blond as the people of the upper Midwest, occa-sionally dashed in its center with green patches of low-lying dandelions, pig-ears, cheat, clover, and foxtail. The road not only swings handsomely along the ridge, it dips and rises, each change offering a different vista across the hills into the woods and trimly farmed valleys below.

Only one sharp angle turns right just past Jake Yant's farmhouse near the mailboxes; then it resumes its easy meandering for another mile until it crosses a line of trees and brush swarming over an old barbed wire fence that marks our boundary. The first part of the road leading to the mailboxes is at least a century old. But the next mile and a half, crossing our boundary and coming to the house, is probably no more than thirty years old. It was put in along some footpaths and cart roads by the township when our place was first built by Eino Paasikivi.

For a decade we drove up to the ridge from Iowa City for weekends and holidays. When we came in on the road after the long drive and crossed our line, exultation came into my head like music. Suzanne and Wanda, our Great Dane, heard the tune, too. The dog began piping and singing lightly, becoming so overwhelmed we had to let her out of the car so she could canter on the road joyously behind us for the last half mile.

At one time there were two farms on our land, but the old Finn tore down the derelict houses and outbuildings when he built our house. There are still traces of the two cart roads, which served those original farms, leading down each side of our ridge, one to the highway and the other to the Kickapoo River. At least twice a year I trim the brush and sickle the weeds back on one of them, sawing any trees that have fallen across. I am always reflective when we make our way down these tracks through the woods. I try to imagine the people who used them, struggling up and down the ridge with their loads in fair and hard weather.

Thomas Hardy wrote of an old road in *The Woodlanders*, "The spot is lonely, and when the days are darkening the many gay charioteers now perished who have rolled along the way, the blistered soles that have trodden it, and the tears that have wetted it, return upon the mind of the loiterer."

The road along our ridge has become almost second nature to us—but we never, never take it for granted, always aware of our privilege—to be able to come and go on such a singular passage. The novelist, Ben Logan, lives on the ridge farm he was born in not far from us. He calls his place "Seldom Seen Ridge." This is not a heavily traveled area. Ours is a remote road, and, in the larger scheme of things, sometimes it is forgotten, especially in fair weather when township roadworkers concentrate on preparing the main routes for harsh weather. Sometimes Hutschenreuter Drive becomes a bit washed and scrabbled.

I was driving home on County Highway C from an errand in Soldiers Grove when I saw one of the township graders working on the berm. I stopped and hailed the driver. He was a young guy, serious in his work, and he reluctantly shut down his blustering motor. I smiled at him and he was surprised and guarded; usually he had to field complaints when he turned off his switch.

"Hey, you're making a lot of noise," I teased him.

"Well, this thing thinks it's a bull," he said, and looked at me again.

I was still smiling. "I just want to thank you for the way you take care of our little road up there—Hutschenreuter Drive."

"What road is that?" he was puzzled.

"Hutschenreuter. H-u-t-s-c-h-e-n-r-e-u-t-e-r."

"Oh yeah, up there," he pointed. "I know where you mean. Big Name road, we call it." He shook his head. He had the smile of a guy who worked hard in all weather. You had to earn it, but when it came, it was genuine.

"That's kind of a lost road," he said. "You doing okay up there?"

"We're doing fine, but it's gotten a little rutted from the rain we've been having. Nothing serious. When you have time, you might want to touch her up."

"I'll get that in," he said. He took off his soiled Milwaukee Brewers cap and scratched his head, peering down at me from his cab. "You been around here long?"

"Only about five years fulltime. I like it a lot. I don't remember anymore what the hell I did with the long part of my life."

He gave me another of his smiles. "It's nice country. Even the winters."

"Cold and snow are what keeps the rabble out."

He gave a honk at this. "You got that right. Amen!" he said. He reached for his switch—it was time to get back to work.

It wasn't an hour later, Sheba started barking and the grader appeared on the rise, sweeping down past my writing shack as it raised a track of tawny dust all the way to the house. I stepped out from the shack to wave to him on his way back out, and he gave me his smile; raised his Brewers cap to me.

ᴥ

Every two or three years the township does new grading, bringing in loads of gravel to spread, especially in low spots where water gathers. The gravel is a crush taken from local quarries, mostly sedimentary stone and bits of crystalline rocks. As we walk in daylight we find treasures in the mix, sparkling fragments of geodes, bits of petrified bone, sharp pieces of pale limestone, and sandstone pocked where ancient vegetation and insects were trapped. At night in starlight or when the moon is up, the pebbles and small rocks are partially illuminated and the road glows with a subtle aura. We do not have to carry a flashlight on our nocturnal rambles, even when the sky is overcast and the darkness total. We know the road.

In spring and fall it becomes glutinous and rutted, but in winter it freezes and hardens. Snow dusts the gravel at first, then drifts high in the winds. We discover who our animal neighbors are when snow covers the road. Tracks of the nonhibernators—deer, mice, rabbits, voles, wild turkeys, and coyotes—crisscross our road and in some places there is a veritable traffic jam of markings.

The snow deepens, but still, as we look out from our house at the drifts, we know where the road is buried and it makes us feel secure. Big Dave Pugh, driver of the township snowplow, knows where it is, too. In time he sweeps in, spraying snow off in each direction as he approaches the house like a ship against the tide, clearing the road for our passage, smiling and waving to us as he swings past the windowed doorway of our library. We put on boots, scarves, and heavy coats, and walk out on our cleared road.

In any season the road called Hutschenreuter is one of our manifest pleasures. We have created paths and trails leading off it into the meadows and steep woods for our rambles, but in deep snowy weather the road is our main vein (not artery—we always think of it more as a coming than a going). Even when woods and fields are sopped with rain or buried in snow, we walk the road and gaze across the meadows through bare trees, down into the valley, and far off to distant wooded ridges where silos, houses, and steeples of country churches notch the sky.

For years we lived in the middle of towns and cities. When finally we came to the ridge fulltime and drove down the road with the last load of our possessions, we were still uncertain about living so remotely. But in a very brief time we felt secure in our permanent solitude. When visitors come in on our road for the first time, they are surprised by the long drive, and then by the vista from our ridge. They park near our house, and we watch from the window as they stand, looking out and listening to the stillness before they approach our door.

Our road leads to silence, but it leads to words as well. Each morning I walk the gravel up the rise to the shack where I write and whisper to myself in the quiet. There are also the words we chatter on our walks, and the words we say to neighbors when we meet them on Hutschenreuter Drive and stand together, sharing tidings of harvests and gardens, changes in the weather, the movement of deer, hawks, and harriers over the meadows.

There have been other important roads in our lives. Years ago there was a road in upper western Pennsylvania that we felt certain was the permanent passage to the center of our abiding spirits, running between fields, through pines and hardwood forest, to a small red cabin near Clarion. When, in the ferment of a long working life, we had to eventually give up this cherished place, we were totally distracted, worried that we would never find another such road in our lives, that we had forsaken a portion of our souls.

But now we have another road. We have walked it in health and happiness. We have walked it in sickness, seeking health. We have walked it in anger until the road has lead us to forgiveness. If I ever pray, I pray on the road. We have been afraid on the road, for our lives and for our world, but the road brings us back to precious aloneness and silence.

After a rare night out, when we drive back in on the road, two miles under starlight, moonlight, or heavy darkness, our solitude is emphasized. The road brings us home to ourselves, and we rejoice that we might be able to finish in such a place.

Part Four ～

I think I could turn and live with animals,
they are so placid and self-contained;
I stand and look at them long and long.
 —Walt Whitman, *Song of Myself*

Ivory

I am absorbed by the resonance and infinite variety of human faces. Over the years, my fascination has taken various forms. As a boy I gathered large collections of baseball cards. When I grew older it was portraits of jazz musicians—then later, engravings and photographs of poets and writers.

But I cherish the unwritten biographical hints of anonymous portraits as well. Some years ago a friend showed me a daguerreotype and I fell hard for those luminous, mid-nineteenth-century faces, scraping up money to track down new treasures in antique stores and hounding dealers for new acquisitions. At one point I had almost three hundred daguerreotypes. Eventually I sold them to buy a truck for our farm. It was a necessary, painful irony. I opened each of the small leather cases and gazed at the shimmering faces as I packed them in boxes to send to the buyer. I felt perfidious and ashamed. I often think of those venerable faces and miss them.

In recent years my passion has become the painted portrait miniatures that were limned in watercolors on small ovals and squares before photography took over portraiture in the mid-nineteenth century. But I am retired now and cannot afford much of this passion. Only rarely am I able to buy one of these captivating objects. But I gaze at them in books and study the few that I possess, trying to learn from them. Again, it is the human faces that I love. Even at this distance, these small portraits create an almost sensuous bond between the painter, subject, and beholder.

I have one fetching early-nineteenth-century portrait of a French bride holding a bouquet, painted on a three-inch ivory oval. She has a veil over her hair, but the artist has skillfully rendered the curls on her forehead and flowers in her arms. Her eyes are luminous brown and she gazes confidently at the viewer. Her hands are gloved and her décolletage is sweet and delicate. Even after two centuries, I sense her allurement—a physical attraction that cannot be denied.

These painted miniatures, ranging from one to four inches across, were rendered with great diligence, at first on vellum or card, with thin brushes and hairs. But in the early decades of the eighteenth century the preferred medium became ivory. It is curious why the artists decided to make this switch. Finished ivory has a lovely translucency, but it is smooth, nonporous, and does not accept watercolor well. It also dries out and sometimes cracks or splits in extreme temperatures, but it is precious material and must have seemed appropriate as a base for this delicate art.

The artists lightly sanded the ivory discs to make them more receptive to the watercolors, and they used an intricate hatching technique of crossed or parallel lines when they painted, or sometimes stippled the colors in small dots. It was demanding work, requiring a quiet mind, steadiness, fine eyes, and a magnifier. Only the well-to-do could afford to have their miniatures painted, and the best examples are subtle and exquisite.

But here an incongruity becomes evident, and my delectation with these minute paintings of human faces goes askew. The delicate wafers of ivory were sliced from the tusks of the most ponderous land mammals in the world—massive African elephants, slaughtered in abundance during the eighteenth and nineteenth centuries to meet the demand for this precious material. Ivory was also used for jewelry, billiard balls, piano keys, and was even ground up to create aphrodisiacs.

It was the search for ivory, rather than slaves, which took coastal East Africans increasingly further into the interior of the continent, but slavery and its evils were inevitably connected to the ivory trade. To hunt elephants one needed guns and ammunition, which could also be used to conquer and enslave. Portage was needed for the loads of huge tusks. The transport of ivory was thus performed by slaves who were seized violently from their interior homelands and sold to coastal shopkeepers and tribal chiefs. The journeys from the elephant hunting grounds to the Ivory Coast were long and cruel. The animals were relentlessly slaughtered, their tusks sawed off and carcasses abandoned to jackals, hyenas, and vultures.

Young George Orwell describes with heartbreaking clarity the fall of a renegade elephant he had been compelled to shoot while serving as a police officer in Burma: "A mysterious, terrible change had come over the elephant. He neither stirred nor fell, but every line of his body had altered. He looked suddenly stricken, shrunken, immensely old, as though the frightful impact of the bullet had paralyzed him without knocking him down. At last, after what seemed a long time—it might have been five seconds, I dare say—he sagged flabbily to his knees. His mouth slobbered. An enormous senility seemed to have settled upon him. One could have imagined him thousands of years old."

Last summer Suzanne and I attended a small circus in Gays Mills, Wisconsin, and watched three performing elephants. When they lumbered into the ring, they seemed like congenial, wizened veterans. Their tusks had been filed back. A blond woman sat on the back of one of them in a spangled sarong, beaming and presenting her dramatic circus wave to the crowd. The elephants' trainer had them stand on stools, parade around the ring, do a dance shuffle, and place their huge front legs on the backs of each other as they stood in a row. They seemed well treated and knew their drill perfectly.

They paraded, swinging their trunks, sometimes touching them to the ground; the small, moist eyes on each side of their heads seemed unaware of us—or uncaring as we applauded on the planks just above them. They looked only at each other, but they seemed willing and entirely cooperative. I noticed that the handlers spoke gently to them as they performed, and wondered if, beyond the practice of their routine, they had private, affectionate moments with the elephants, as one might with beloved pets.

The elephants require a tremendous amount of work. They have no sweat glands and clean themselves by picking up trunkfuls of dirt and scrubbing it into their tough, almost hairless skin. Then, they must be hosed off and made presentable for their performances. They eat five hundred pounds of hay and grain and drink fifty gallons of water a day, sucking it into their trunks and squirting it into their mouths. In the wild they smash down whole trees to eat their canopies.

These Asian circus elephants were about eight or nine feet tall at their shoulders. When they noiselessly paraded into the ring, their grace was surprising and their smell quickly evident—the odor of great animals, earthy, urinous, elephantine, not offensive, but entirely evident. During one part of the act they were asked to lie down and slowly reclined onto their sides to rest beside each other. They seemed so sweet and vulnerable in this position. They closed their eyes—playing dead elephants—and when they were asked to rise, they seemed reluctant and sleepy, struggling at last to lift their great bodies until they were on their feet again. There is a famous photograph of an escaped, exhausted elephant lying on its side in the distance on a country road, surrounded by emergency vehicles and fire trucks hosing down its dehydrated body. It is a melancholy, telling image. The elephant has its head down in the dark stains of water on the pavement and its wild flight is finished. It had obviously escaped from a circus and rambled a long way.

When circus trains came to Canton in the 1940s, my father would awaken me before dawn and we would drive to a railroad siding to watch the unloading. The folded canvases, apparatus for the acts, animal cages, and large shipping cases were rolled onto wagons and transported to the grounds. The powerful, dependable elephants helped with these operations and moved the wagons to the circus grounds. When the big tent poles were rigged, elephants pulled the ropes to raise the heavy canvas into place.

After watching this, Dad and I would go home for breakfast; then in the afternoon he and my mother would take me to the midway and the big top show. Circuses were a great treat for my father. He would take one of his rare days off to attend. He told me that when he was a boy he often volunteered to help the workers when the circus came to town and they would let him fetch and tote light loads.

Now he worked fifty hours a week in a store. When we came home from our day at the circus he needed to rest. He was not a big man and had a curvature of the spine. When he napped, he laid on his side. In this position he seemed at peace and sweetly vulnerable. I'd stay in the room, quietly playing, pretending that I was watching over and protecting him. Sometimes I'd go up close to look at him sleeping and listen to his breathing, gazing at his eyelids quivering as he dreamed. It wasn't authority I felt, but I liked believing that I had responsibility for him as he rested on his side.

Sheba, our dog and sweet friend. I am looking at her at this very moment as I write in my shack. She is on her side near me—not asleep, but in the twilight zone of dogs. It is a summer day and she is panting slightly. She is waiting for me to finish my work, being patient, doing what dogs do so well—being *with* me. Occasionally she stretches and sticks out her front legs, straightening her neck. Then she dozes some more. If I reach down to pet her she lifts her head for a moment to look at me, to see if this might be *the* moment she is waiting for, when we head back to the house. There is a painting of a small girl holding her dog in one of my books on portrait miniatures. The dog looks exactly like Sheba. The note says that this is a two-inch British watercolor portrait, rendered on ivory approximately two centuries ago.

Sheba is ten years old now and there is not much I can do that will surprise her. But as I type a handwritten draft of this piece into my word processor, I discover that the entry for "elephant" in the computer encyclopedia has a recording of an elephant trumpeting. I push this on and the mighty squall makes Sheba stand up and look about. She has never heard an elephant trumpeting. I have no idea what she is envisioning, but clearly this is a sound to be reckoned with.

Elephants live about as long as a human will live. The oldest elephant ever known, Lin Wang, died recently in a zoo in Taiwan at the age of eighty-six. In the wild, their herds of ten or fifteen members are led by ancient matriarchs. They rarely give birth in captivity. They do not choose to come with humans, as dogs will do, but when we capture them and prove that we can be trusted, they gently coexist with us. They doze sometimes as they stand, but sleep deeply on their sides like dogs or fathers.

They are still illegally slaughtered and now the poachers carry battery-driven chainsaws to remove their tusks. The United Nations recently voted to lift the prohibition on the sale of stockpiled ivory, which had been included in the international ban on hunting elephants. Animal protectionists believe that this will create new demands for ivory and encourage further illegal poaching.

There are probably fewer than 500,000 elephants left in the world. Twenty years ago there were twice that many. Centuries ago there were millions, and before that they walked every landmass in the world.

The Gray Fox

Families, dogs, kids fuzzed with cotton candy, temporary whirligigs and merry-go-rounds crowd the grounds of Beauford T. Anderson Park. It is Dairy Days in Soldiers Grove, and the streets of the little town are lined with pickup trucks and RVs. On the rise above the green is the Lions Club Pavilion, where the brotherhood serves bratwurst, hotdogs, battered smelts, French fries, and dripping cans of soft drink and beer from ice tubs. A slow-pitch softball tournament plugs along in a field below the shelter, and the infielders are chattering. Down near the road ponderous tan and gray horses are prepared to pull weighted sleds; drivers exercise their draft pairs at the edge of a corral fence.

Richie Halverson and I sit in the wooden bleachers, watching the horses bob their heads and toss up clods with their hooves as they wait for the events to get started. I have just told Richie about the gray fox I saw in our woods this morning.

I was coming against the wind as I walked the old farm road to the double meadows, and I surprised the fox in a damp draw as he was trying to root out some small animal from a rusty drainpipe under the road. Foxes usually hunt at night, and grays are rare in our area. Both of us were surprised. He glanced at me for a moment before running, and I saw that his salt-and pepper-coat was spotted with sludge. He looked scrawny and harassed, being out in the daylight, and he scurried off into the blackberry bushes and prickly ash.

"A gray fox. Is that a fact?" Richie says. "Gray fox used to be all through here before coyotes got so thick. I ain't seen one in thirty years, I'll bet. You sure it was a gray?"

"It had a black stripe down its tail and it was rusty on its neck and feet."

"Yep. Sounds like a gray to me, all right. When did I see one last time?" Richie can be discursive when he starts a story, sometimes challenging you with sudden changes of subject and chronological side roads. But when he respects his tale and isn't bored by it, he takes his time and spins it slowly to make sure you get all the parts.

"It was in the seventies, I guess. Some hippies came out of Madison and built a little shack out of crate-wood on one of my far forties without even asking. I had to tell 'em to move on, and they gave me some sass about how the earth belonged to everyone. But they were trying to grow marijuana, and they were building fires in the woods. I thought they were going to burn down all my trees. They were just fuzzy kids—a girl and two boys—but I couldn't have 'em in there.

"When they finally got out, they left their shack standing. The door fell off after a while and animals took up the place. Some foxes moved in, and I saw they were grays.

"I was out hunting rabbits and came up on the place where the shack was. I saw the foxes were raising a litter inside. I let 'em be and went on with my business. Late in the afternoon I looked down from the ridge, and there were coyotes sneaking up. They rustled that family out and jumped on 'em fast. Of course the babies and mama went first. The old guy tried to make a stand for 'em."

Richie paused here, and his eyes lowered behind his silver-rimmed spectacles. "I got to hand it to him. He was up there on his hinders, showing his teeth and slashing. He was doing all he could do. But a gray can't hold against those devils. They were too much, and he went down, too. Coyotes were chewin' on all of 'em. It didn't take long, and there was nothing I could do. Grays lived in this country a long time, but I never seen one after that. It's good you saw him, but I don't think he'll last long."

The public address system kicks on suddenly, blaring over the bleachers. "Testing, one-two. Testing."

Richie and I are watching the horse teams exercise when he slaps his thick hand to his cheek and knocks his glasses askew.

"By God, there's Cork Benson! I thought he was down for the count. He's going to pull again!" We look at a bulky man with curly gray hair fuzzing out from his Milwaukee Brewers cap. He is listing hard to one side, leaning on a carved stick as he watches a pair of bay horses with heavily feathered legs.

Richie turns to me confidentially. "Everybody knows Cork around here. He's part horse himself. Back in the early fifties he brought a kickoff back eighty-six yards, and we won the "B" championship. The only time for Soldiers Grove. Nobody ever forgot it. I was a freshman guard, trying to block for him, but he like to knock me down as he run by. Nobody was going to stop him. Cork could *go*. He got hurt farming a while back. Now he's got the arthritis."

Cork is not exercising his own horses like the other participants. He watches as a handler works his team. With the lead straps wrapped around their arms, drivers walk on their heels like heavy ducks against the pull of the horses. The men are thick and broad-shouldered, but none so imposing as Cork Benson.

There is one woman driver in a red, XXXL T-shirt with her hair tucked up under her cap. She has enough substance to lay back on the straps and make up for what the men have in brawn. She keeps to herself, but at the end, after many rounds, she is standing among the prizewinners.

These are serious people with a heritage—sons and daughters, grandsons and granddaughters of old draft-horse pullers. There aren't many left, and it is difficult to get enough drivers and horses together for a contest. As they waddle behind their huge pairs toward the gray, weighted sled, the drivers are joined by two handlers wearing heavy work gloves. These "hookers" take up grips on each side of a clanging metal "evener bar" that drags on chains behind the team. Just before the pull they attach the bar with an eye bolt to a hook on the front of the sled. Sometimes these hookers chat amiably as they walk toward the sled, but the driver never speaks except to his horses.

Mostly Belgians and a few gray mottled Percherons, these imposing horses are a resonance of power from long ago. They have wide, white stripes down their noses and their thick manes are crew cut. They belong to the muscular earth, the open fields and wooded hills. With one move they could smash a human, but they remain stoic and focused behind their blinders. If they had been graced with only a few more brain cells, they would be in charge of the earth, driving these brawny men to task in the late afternoon sun of this pleasant Wisconsin summer day. Their tack and harness are elaborate with many buckles and rings; the harness extends under their front legs and around their heavy necks and is studded with brightly burnished silver. The horses know their strength and are anxious for the task. The bleachers are full of experienced watchers, a crowd that knows enough to remain silent until after the pull is completed, so that the horses do not become excited.

A sprightly, knowledgeable, one-armed man on the public-address system announces the participants as they come to the sled with their teams. "Jim Bergum and his brother, Bob, they been pulling for a long time. Their Dad, Augie, pulled for many years before them," he tells the crowd. "Augie's sitting in the stands now. Give the Bergums a nice hand, folks."

A stalwart young woman with bobbed hair stands near the sled with the judges and handlers, holding a stopwatch. The pulls are not timed, but she keeps track of any delays that might occur, allowing two minutes for any repairs, and helps the men slide the 150-pound concrete slabs from the tractor wagon onto the sled when more weight is added.

"Looka that Annie Olson, folks, working right in there with the men," the public-address announcer says. "Let's give her a hand."

The horse pairs are walked to the front of the sled and, with much shouting and tugging, are backstepped to the hookup. Already they anticipate their task, straining and stomping their heavy hooves, flexing the muscles of their shoulders and thighs, poised to explode with power. The driver, holding the reins, plunks down on a bench on the sled. The hookers must quickly set the evener eyebolt onto the sled hook. If things are not done correctly at this point, there is danger of serious injury to themselves or to the drivers—smashed fingers, a dislocated shoulder or elbow, a fractured skull.

When the hitch is made, the handlers leap aside as the driver shouts, "Get up!" There is a mighty bashing and clanking as the horses lunge forward, their hindquarters digging, making divots fly, pushing with force so the forelegs can reach out and set again, thrusting forward so their hinders reset to continue driving the body onward. The horses

sometimes go down almost to their knees when they first heave themselves against the dead weight, but the muscles of their rear legs propel
them on and up again. The force and moment are riveting. Even Richie,
who has seen dozens of these events over the years, is excited. "It's the
chest and the back legs," he marvels. "That's the power."

The weight on the sled is increased for each round. The horses must
drag the load a minimum of 27.5 feet to be eligible to move on. They
have three tries to make it. Teams that falter are eliminated. Light
horse teams generally end up pulling more than three tons to win their
competition, and larger horses, each weighing more than thirty-two-
hundred pounds, sometimes pull up to four tons. The program sheet
says, "A representative of the State Humane Office, or a local humane
officer, may be present at any contest." It also says at the bottom, in the
Wisconsin tradition, BEER TENT ON GROUNDS.

The winner of the contest gets ninety dollars. Second prize is eighty
dollars, and so on down through seven prizes. Competition is intense.
A furious, red-shirted driver comes out from behind the corral fence
and shouts at the handlers of a faltering team. They have been stalled
because their bridles and straps have slipped, and the handlers are
struggling to set them straight.

Red Shirt bellows at them, "Two minutes! That's all you get to
reset them straps. Two minutes is up. Them's the rules. Get your horses
out of there."

But the handlers of the stalled horses, and Annie Olson with the
stopwatch, ignore him until the rig is properly adjusted. Everyone seems
a little nonplussed by Red Shirt's bad manners. It is an easy afternoon
in southwestern Wisconsin, a festival day, and everyone wants to see
the pull. Red Shirt goes mumbling back to his horses.

A team of matched Belgians slams into its pull, and the tip of the
heavy sled hook breaks off under the strain. The horses are suddenly
dashing free across the corral, dragging the driver behind. Somehow
he manages to unwrap, lets go of the reins, and goes spinning in the
dust. We all come to our feet in alarm as the horses pitch toward a line
of people standing near the far fence. They scramble to get out of the
way and men rush out from the crowd to try to grasp the reins. The

loose horses charge through the corral gate toward where the other horses are tied and, as suddenly as they started, come to rest among their own kind.

The men get up and dust themselves off. No one is hurt. Everyone is chuckling; the feeling of relief is palpable. Two handlers haul out a large toolbox and work at the base of the battered wooden sled to set a new hook. As they bang and sweat, the public-address announcer switches on and says, "You boys want some duct tape?" Everyone laughs some more. Across the road from the corral, the parking area is full of brightly polished, souped-up tractors of all sizes, painted with names and slogans like "No Fear" and "Hell's Challenger." They are ready to roar and whine through the evening's feature: a tractor-pulling competition. But this sweet Wisconsin afternoon belongs to the great horses.

A few weeks before, while shopping in the local co-op hardware store, I listened to two older farmers talking. It was a hot day, and they were pulling bolts from the bins to make tractor repairs. "I hate to get down under that thing when I'm sweating like this, but what are you going to do? She's down."

"Just remember the old days, Cal. This is easier than horses."

"I ain't so sure." Cal's face was glazed and crimson, one of his thick forearms marked by a deep, fork-shaped scar. "We didn't have much then, but them might have been better days in the long run. A horse falls down, but it gets itself back up. I never cussed a horse, but a lot of days I end up cussing my goddamned tractor."

Cork Benson is scheduled to pull. We all wait for him as he painfully moves his bulk, bearing down on his cane with a slow, cantilevered walk toward the weighted sled. His Brewers cap is pulled down tight to the top of his capacious nose, shading his red-rimmed, azure eyes. The public-address announcer does not need to say his name. Everybody knows Cork.

As he makes his way, the wind rustles up slightly over the valley, raising some powder from the corral and giving momentary relief from the heat. A few of the tractor drivers from across the way have grown bored with waiting for the evening events and gone off to a side street to tool up their vehicles, making their tires howl on the pavement.

When Cork finally sits down on the bench, a strapping young man, perhaps his son, leads the horses around with the hookers and deferentially hands the reins to Cork.

The hookers quickly make the connection and step back. Cork shakes the reins, but his "get-up" shout is barely a wheeze. The horses, waiting for authority, move almost casually, barely leaning against the weight of the sled. Cork leans forward in the bench and hisses his command again, but the horses only shake their shoulders and snort lightly. They flex their legs, stand still and gaze off at the surrounding hills as if embarrassed. They are waiting for the arresting command of Cork Benson, but it does not come.

Together for some silent moments in the lowering light, the man and his horses are in silhouette to the crowd in the bleachers. At last Annie Olson with the bobbed hair indicates Cork's time is up. He has done all that he can do. The handlers quickly unhitch his horses and lead them away. Cork climbs down from the scuffed sled bench and, bent like a fishhook, hobbles through the silence to where his horses are waiting behind the corral fence.

The Mechanics

An eyesore, my mother called it. Neighborhood legend had it that the building was originally a bootleg operation disguised as a pickle factory; but in the late 1930s Art Saunier acquired it and changed it into an auto repair shop. I was a child, and hence Art's Garage seemed to me a place of true significance when I played near it in our quiet neighborhood. It was a long, tan, stucco building in the middle of our block of tidy frame houses, extending all the way back from McGregor Avenue to the alley called Rose Court, and it seemed like a cave through the summer brightness.

When the world war started, Art closed it down and went to serve in the army paratroopers. He was severely wounded in Sicily and received an early discharge. He came home walking with a limp, his right cheek and jaw mangled, and his eye drooping in a perpetual wince. I remembered almost nothing of Art before he went away, but my father said he had been steady and strong. Now he talked with a lisp and sometimes his hands shook.

Two large, sagging doors hung at the entry to the garage, at the end of a concrete ramp running up from our street. There were glass-block windows along each side of the building, with hinged prop panels in the middle. Inside, the long building was divided into three open rooms. The front part was Art's work area—benches, jacks, pull-lights, heavy wrenches, screwdrivers, rubber hammers. In the middle bay Art parked junked vehicles that he stripped for parts, and the back room was where he discarded useless, impossible junk. Art never threw anything away. He kept a space open in the middle of this third room, and all around the walls he piled greasy, mechanical flotsam and jetsam.

"You never know," he would say.

He was a messy, eccentric mechanic. There were pools and smears of oil on the filthy cement. Broken gearwheels, shafts, and piston rods were tossed into corners until he had time to transfer them to the back room. But apparently Art knew his stuff. Our neighbor, Ron Flynn, said, "He's good. That man can zip a busted motor back up and make it sing again." Art's business was brisk, and often he worked late into the night.

My father took a stroll each evening after supper to smoke a cigar, and usually I walked with him. We often stepped into the garage on our way home to chat with Art as he worked. He kept a heavy, oil-stained wooden bench in his repair area for visitors. As a rule, there were two or three neighborhood men hanging around or playing poker. Art was under a jacked-up car or had his head under a hood and rarely joined in these conversations, but he seemed to enjoy having his garage serve as a kind of neighborhood evening men's club.

Art's war wounds seemed frightful to me. On summer days I would sometimes wander into the garage to say hello to him and find him slumped on the sitting bench with his head in his hands. He was very lean, and when he raised his head, in the dim light from the glass-block windows, the shadows were deep in his eye sockets and across his wounded cheek. He wore a filthy engineer's cap on his unwashed gray hair. He sighed often and did not look at you when he talked. My father said that Art had a girlfriend when he went away to war, but she married someone else while he was gone. Now that he was so badly hurt, it didn't seem possible that a woman would have him. I never saw him smile. Occasionally he would fake a cackle when one of the men told a joke, but he kept his mouth rigid when he laughed.

When I looked in on Art during the day, if he had a moment and was in the mood, he would try to explain some of the work he was doing. He asked me to help him by turning a screw or bolt. As I did this, he carefully explained and assured me that what I was doing made a difference, holding two parts together or tightening an important connection. With his greasy fingers he would draw with a pencil stub pictures and diagrams on the back of old bill forms to illustrate connections and working parts.

But I was a small boy, and I never understood how the engines worked. He could see this, but he kept trying to instruct me, and he was a good, earnest teacher. Finally, I would say, "Mr. Saunier, I've got to go now."

On one side of Art's garage building was a house, but the other side faced a vacant lot full of tall grass and weed trees. This was sacred ground to me. I had buried my pet rabbit, Mortimer, in this soil. I knew a stray cat who hunted the weeds. She was very strange and skittish and accepted only me as her friend. One summer I cleared a patch of weeds and constructed a wooden hut from orange crates that I purloined from Volzer's Grocery. I built it beneath cooling ailanthus trees, propping it against the garage under one of the glass-block windows. I kept it stocked with comics, forbidden matchbooks, and candle stubs I had pocketed from the wastebasket in St. John's sacristy when I served mass. I thumbtacked a picture of Jim Hegan, the Cleveland Indians' catcher, on the rough boards. It was my secret place. I could hear Art inside, talking to himself and clanking his tools.

I got into a scrap with my playmates one August afternoon and retreated to my secret hut. My mother had given me a worn-out bed pillow, and I propped myself up, nibbled some Good 'n' Plenties from a Mason jar, and lit one of my candle stubs. It was very quiet in the semi-dark, with only grasshoppers grating the summer heat in the field and the stray cat purring as I stroked it. I had just begun turning the pages of a *Boy Commandos* comic when I heard a sound that began like a pennywhistle, descending abruptly to a growl, trailing off into a wail, then breaking into sobs. It came once more, the pattern repeated—then again, this alarming sound like a great angry bird, again, then again. I bumped my head as I tried to stand up, then scrambled out of the hut. I stood in the high sunlight of the field, knee deep in broomgrass and cheat, rubbing my head. The wailing went on and on, echoing from the window of Art's Garage, the sound making me feel desolate and frightened.

I ran through the weeds to the front of the building and peered into the big open doorway, into the long darkness extending through the three rooms all the way back to Rose Court. The howling was coming from the rear of the building.

I thought to go for help, but this would take time. There was an urgency in the calling. I stepped into the dank light of the garage and crept back and back, through the work area, the stacks of worn tires, crisscross of greasy shafts and gears, tools scattered about the pitted cement, the smell of ancient engines and burnt-out gears, into the next room of derelict Fords, Chevrolets, and Dodges that Art had stripped down for parts. Then into the last room, the room of chaos, the space where abandoned, totally useless things had been thrown into corners, smelling of rust, encrusted carbon, and rotting rubber.

Art was in the open space in the middle of the junk piles, pacing with a violent motion, holding his head as he reeled back and forth in the light coming through the glass-block window. His howling had not varied, the shrill cry, grinding into a coarse growl that ended in a wail. His mouth stayed open, his eyes seemed lidless as he limped back and forth. I thought he might be trying to kill himself with his squalling.

I wanted to bolt from this room of anguish; more than anything I had ever felt—I wanted to flee. But if I ran, who would help Art? I cannot say why I held my ground. A small boy. Perhaps I felt pity—an obscure thing for a child to feel—but it was a concern that overcame my uncertainty and terror.

"Mr. Saunier," I said tentatively. He did not stop his wailing.

"Mr. Saunier, are you hurt?"

He paused then, lowered his hands from his head and looked about. When he saw me he looked away. His mouth loosened. He wrung his hands and blinked. "Oh," he murmured. He closed his eyes, but he was quiet.

"Are you okay?" I asked.

He looked at me again; then his eyes rolled up into his head. "Oh."

I thought he might fall. I took a step toward him and reached out. "Have you hurt yourself?" He saw my hand and took hold of it with his heavy, blackened fingers.

"Can I do anything?" I asked. He did not squeeze my hand, but held it almost greedily and breathed hard with his eyes shut. The scars were stark and jagged on his face.

"Is everything okay?"

He nodded his head, then let go of my hand.

"Can I get something for you? Should I get help?"

He shook his head. He said nothing, but I felt that he was all right now. He would be able to go on. Somehow I had helped him. I knew this. I started backing toward the big open doorway. But before I could bolt, he held up his stained hand, flat toward me, and moved it back and forth, like a priest giving a blessing. He opened his eyes wide and looked at me, shook his head gently, as if pleading.

I knew what he wanted. I never told anyone—not my parents, my friends, my schoolmates. Like the secret grave of my dead rabbit, this episode became part of the arcane life I led sometimes in the field beside the garage. The image of Art's soiled fingers on the paper as he drew diagrams, and his words of instruction remain in my mind.

But I have never been able to repair my own engines; their workings have remained a mystery to me. Years later I was a desperate young man when a feverishly enthusiastic woman at a San Francisco employment agency called me about a position she had just listed. "Here it is, Paul. Your writing job. Go get it!" Her zeal was understandable—if I was hired I had promised her agency half my first month salary. I could little afford this, but I had been drudging for a year as a clerk for a stockbroker after leaving college, and my boredom was comprehensive.

At the job interview, Roland Persons peered at me over the top of his glasses. "The writing we do is not very creative. I was an English major, too. This isn't poetry; it's more like laying bricks."

"But I want a job where I can work with words."

"Do you know anything about cars?"

"A little," I lied.

"We don't exactly write about Elysian Fields here."

But I was young, and possibilities seemed unlimited. I figured I could make it work. Poets have special powers. I would apply my talents to the gears.

National Automotive Services published a basic car repair manual and a subscription service to annual supplements for new model cars as they were produced. Their offices were in a derelict building in a cheap rental district near the docks, where the air smelled of sour wine and spoiled French fries. When we came to work in the morning, we often found winos sleeping it off on the front steps of the building.

Sometimes they tried to enter our office, and it was one of my duties to usher them back to the street. "Brother!" they would say to me as I moved them toward the door. "A cigarette. A quarter."

Roland Persons was a kind man, but he had his own responsibilities, and there was work to be done. Very quickly he realized that I did not know the difference between a camshaft and a sparkplug. My mechanical obtuseness had appeared early in life, and it was unlikely that I would ever be able to make the connections. Sometimes the owner lost patience with me, but Roland would cover for me, giving reassurances that I was making progress. He tried to nurse me along. He drew pictures and diagrams for me and tried to hone down my florid, ambitious prose. We gleaned and standardized our repair copy from the new model manuals issued by the manufacturers. Roland was right—it was like masonry with words, but I could never quite get things to line up plumb.

When I worked at National Automotive there must have been mechanics in Peoria and Albany and San Luis Obispo and Macon tearing out their hair. Sometimes the office received outraged phone calls. Finally Roland called me into his office. "The heat is really on," he said. "Don't quit until you have another job, but don't take more than two weeks to find one."

Since those days, I have had even greater respect for the work of mechanics, and I regard their mysterious rituals as blessings. I have benefited from these mercies in some very remote places.

It was an alien scene at dusk, like driving on a moonscape, halfway between the Atomic Energy Commission base at Mercury, Nevada, and the checkpoint at the border of the test-grounds, before the road went on across the desert to our army camp called Desert Rock. I was returning from a briefing in Mercury when my open jeep suddenly wheezed and started missing. Then it went ping, and something snapped. I steered it onto the shoulder and sat hunched over the wheel, listening to the silence. The sun was almost down and a chill wind lowered with the darkness, blowing off the snow-patched desert hills in the distance. I was wearing only a lightweight fatigue jacket. The temperature had been warm when I left Desert Rock that morning, but the briefing had gone on and on through the day.

I climbed out and threw up the hood, staring numbly at the cooling motor. There was nothing I could do. Nothing. I sat down on the bumper and cursed.

These had been strange, challenging months for me, an ongoing phantasm of fear and absurdity—fireballs and mushroom clouds, shock waves burying me in trenches, my bed blown away by violent sandstorms, my ears set permanently ringing by huge explosions. I had been alternately bored by soporific duties and frightened to my limit.

Now here I was in the middle of another nightmare, broken down and alone as stygian darkness advanced across the desert. I looked each way up and down the road and saw some lights in the distance. There was nothing to do but button my jacket, pull my cap down to my nose, jam my hands into my pockets, and hoof it down the packed macadam toward the glow. Whatever these lights might be, they were my best hope, an extraordinary piece of luck, because for forty-five minutes as I drove the road, I had not passed another vehicle nor seen anything along the dismal way but sand, brittle-bush, yucca, and violently authoritative warning signs posted by the AEC.

By the time I reached the lights several miles down the road, I had almost turned blue. But I was relieved to find that they came from the camp of a small army engineer unit, stationed on the test-grounds to prepare and maintain military viewing areas. The top sergeant took me to a motor pool and introduced me to a mechanic who had just finished his evening chow. I have not forgotten that mechanic's name—it was Danny Winiarski. He was grease from head to toe as he shook my hand; only his teeth were white as he smiled, but to my cold, weary eyes he looked as neat and efficient as an English butler.

"Whatsa trouble?" Danny said. When I told him, he revved up a tow truck and we drove back down the road, hooked up my afflicted vehicle and pulled it back to his repair tent. He threw the hood up and stuck his head under.

"Holy shit!" Danny said. My weary nerves jumped. I had to sit down on an oily stool in his work tent. What Danny said then made no sense at all to me. It was mechanical rant, an automotive litany that sounded something like: "Oh man, the piston's cranked into them fuckin' pipes; it's in the upper manifold. It got throwed against the rods. She's stroking the gears off the intake valve. She's pushing a cylinder into the carburetor. We got to come through the throttle. We got to shim the drive wheel to the spark plug. I ain't got the right fuckin' coil spring. But I think we can persuade her."

"Jesus!" I said. "I hope so."

"We'll get her," Danny said. He had a kerosene heater in his garage tent, and I huddled near it as he tied into the job with his tools. I noticed he kept a can of beer going, which he hid in a coffee tin in case the sergeant walked in. He ran a monologue as he worked. "The fuckin' engineers who dreamed up jeeps had brains made out of pinto beans. There ain't no wrench made that can get to some of these nuts, and then you got to have an arm shaped like a Z. You can't even get the hood up without skinning a knuckle. What you need is dynamite and glue to repair these things."

"I sure do appreciate your help," I said.

"If we can't help each other out here in this shit-hole, what can we do? This ain't no place for a human being. You got sand everywhere, in your eyes, between your teeth, up your asshole. Then the sun goes down, and you can't even tune in a radio. At least you guys got a PX at Desert Rock. All we got at night here is beer and cold stars. I ain't seen a movie in six months. And girls! What are they? I got into Vegas a couple of times, and I got so excited I couldn't get near the tables because I got a rod on the whole time, looking at the women. You want a beer?"

"I don't mind if I do, if you've got enough."

"Beer, I got," he said. "Pussy, I don't." He took an opener out of his toolbox and punctured a can top for me.

"I stay about half-lit most of the time," he said. "It's the only way you can get through this place. When they test them bombs, they got to move us out of here because our camp is so close. Sometimes they make us go into the trenches with you Desert Rock guys."

He started hammering on a ratchet handle and I couldn't hear him for a while, but he didn't stop talking. Finally he got the nut to turn.

"Them bombs come from hell," he was saying. "I never thought I'd see anything like that in my life. Them things were thought up by the evil brothers of the engineers who dreamed up jeeps. Them bastards are going to burn down the whole world if we give 'em half a chance. They don't give a shit about anything but their brains. I bet they all look like pissed-off Frankensteins. What do they care about guys like us? They'd blow our fuckin' heads off, if they thought it would get 'em ahead. I'll never get used to them explosions. Hell, I don't even like to watch fireworks. If I had known this was going to happen to me when they drafted me, I'd of volunteered for the 82d poopy-troopers and jumped out of airplanes. It would have been better than crawling around in trenches waiting to get your ass blowed off. Some of the guys in this outfit pretend they ain't scared. Tough guys. Hell, I don't mind saying that them things make my balls turn cold. What kind of a fool are you, if you can't admit being scared of hell's fire? If I get out of here alive, I'm going to start going to mass again."

After a while I nodded off. Danny poked me awake.

"Go over there and lay down on top of my cot," he said. "Use the extra blanket."

I awakened from time to time to hear him mumbling and clanking his tools. It was first light by the time he finished. He took me by the arm and led me to my jeep, proudly turned the ignition on, and revved the motor for me. I had slept through most of his angelic night ministrations.

"You're on your way," Danny said.

"Listen, man. How can I thank you?"

"Don't worry about that, pal. The U.S. Army is paying for it."

"Let me give you some dough."

"Put that away! I'll tell you what. If you come through here again, bring me a six-pack of Regal Pale."

"Hey! You worked all night while I was sawing logs on your cot. I'm not even in your outfit."

"Pal, we are in this thing together. They stuck us in this shit hole to see how we would stand it. If we can't help each other, what the fuck have we got?"

I did see Danny Winiarski again a month later. It was late morning after we had been brought back on buses to Desert Rock from a dawn test shot. Weary and dazed, we were assembled for a final roll call and briefing. There was Danny, stomping around in the cold with his engineer mates. I went over and touched his shoulder.

"Hey!" he said. "It's the sleeping beauty."

"I owe you something," I said.

"Will you stop that shit!"

"Don't go anywhere until I come back."

The PX had opened and I brought a full case of Regal Pale talls, hustled back to the gathering, and put it on Danny's shoulder.

"What are you doin'?" Danny said. He was embarrassed in front of his buddies. "I don't know this guy," he assured them. He tried to hand the case back to me, but I pushed it back.

"For the cold stars," I said.

"This guy is a stranger," he told his mates. "I don't know him." But he kept the beer.

I remained a mechanical stranger for many years. When I retired to rural Wisconsin and took up grass cutting and gardening, I still had to rely on others to maintain my equipment. Ted Magnuson was a considerate and understanding machinist. The benches and shelves in his repair shop were always lined with torn-down motors that he was resuscitating and bringing back to life. At one time or another Ted had helped everyone in the community through some very tough spots.

I was a short-timer in rural southwestern Wisconsin, and I needed Ted's help more than anyone else. I had learned to do some maintenance and occasionally made simple repairs, but I relied on Ted when my Bolens tractor really started biting back. He even made house calls when I was in particular trouble.

Ted Magnuson had not finished high school, but he was an accomplished man. Sometimes I sat on his bench and hung around just to watch him work. Good mechanics are usually methodical, but Ted went beyond this. He didn't think of shafts and bolts and cogwheels as objects to be lined up and reinstalled in one-two-three order. When he worked on a motor, his eyes deepened, and he seemed to shift into another dimension, an abstract area of matrices, connections, and prototypes, where the parts floated in a loose plane of possibilities, until they came together in his mind and through his agile hands.

He kept a small grease-thumbed portable radio at hand as he worked and tuned it in to the classical station from Madison. One day I walked into his shop as a Mahler symphony was resounding into its second hour, and Ted was under the tractor humming and whistling along with the melodies. I had always hesitated to ask him about his musical preferences, but now I could resist no longer.

"That's interesting music," I said. Ted kicked his heels and rolled out from under the tractor on his flat cart to see who was talking to him, then he gave me his good smile. "Some of my customers say I listen to ghost music."

"Do you play an instrument?"

"Just this radio. I got tired of listening to country when I was a kid. They keep telling the same stories, and I always know the endings. I finally figured music could just be music. Just the sound. Mozart lets me do my own thinking."

Ted was a man of wit, too, a master of the pun and the straight face. His laughter came without reservation. He loved to banter with me. Once I purchased a set of bright orange earguards to wear when I was running my chainsaw. A week later I took them back to his shop.

"Ted," I said, faking perplexity. "I can't get any music to come out of these buggers. I've tried everything."

"Let me see them things," he said. He turned the head set in his hands and deliberated. "I see the trouble. You got to tie a rope to it right here and run it to a tree if you want to get the Mozart."

Sometimes my Bolens defies me, whining and choking off in the middle of a job like a stolid, exasperating child. I dismount and circle it, at first hopeful that the trouble might just be an empty gas tank. I have no compassion or patience for faltering mechanical things. If they break down, I hate them. Failure is unacceptable. As the recognition of real trouble grows, I begin to feel sorry for myself. Why should this idiot thing disappoint me like this? Then I grow angry and kick the fat tires. Stupid, Goddamned thing!

Already I sense the grass growing out of control. I must do something before we disappear in a sea of green. I used to dial Ted like a hysterical patient calling a doctor. I once suggested that he get on the 911 emergency circuit. "You're more important than the fire department," I told him. Ted grew to recognize my symptoms and, like a good doctor, did his best to comfort me. Eventually I'd see his pickup coming patiently over the rise.

"What's wrong with her?" he'd ask.

"She won't run."

"I can see *that*. Did she kick up a fuss or make a noise when she was going down?"

"She sounded like she was going to throw up. Then she farted, screamed once, and just stopped."

"Whoa!" Ted exclaimed. "Oh-oh." He walked around the Bolens and toed the tires as my anxiety rose. "Sounds like the green fantods to me."

"What?" I said in alarm. I was always terrified of some new mechanical plague that might befall my equipment.

"She's got indigestion," he said. "Too many dandelions."

"Come on, Ted! I'm half out of my mind."

"I know that," he said. "I'm just trying to keep you loose." He pulled his tool-chest out of the truck bed, got his greasy little radio from the cab, tuned in the Madison classics, and set to work.

Ted's son, Luke, has the shrouded eyes and bashed-in nose of a parking lot fighter. He is brawnier than his father, but he has the same scuffed mechanic's knuckles. He also has Ted's unqualified laugh—but it comes rarely. Luke seems to be the antithesis of his gentle father. He started hanging around the garage when he was ten, and Ted was a good teacher. But Luke's temperament and approach to the work is different than Ted's. He takes on repairs like he challenges everything else in his life, attacking a broken-down motor as if it were his adversary, flinging tools around on the gummy, black cement, and cursing when he can't make things fit.

Ted Magnuson died one summer of a brain tumor. Suddenly he was gone, and the whole community went into mourning. I went to his crowded funeral and gave my condolences to Luke, but I did not have the heart to go to the shop for a while. I knew what I had lost and could only imagine how Ted's family felt. But finally I drove to town to see how Luke was doing. The shop door was propped open, but there was no one around. I ducked under the counter and walked through the workbenches and parts bins. No one answered my calls. At last I found Luke in the back of the stockroom, slouched behind some shelves on a stack of tractor tires.

He would not look up and could barely respond when I talked to him. I saw how deeply he was mourning—almost beyond the normal grief of a young son for his father. I realized that Ted had not only kept our engines running, he had kept young Luke in repair as well. Now Ted was suddenly gone before the job was completed.

I put a tentative hand on Luke's shoulder and spoke gently. He lifted his head and looked at me squarely. I took a step back. I quickly realized where I stood. I needed Luke now, but Luke did not need me. Luke needed his father—and his father was gone. He didn't want anyone else trying to be fatherly. His father was irreplaceable. I was going to have to remember this. Luke did not want to banter with me; I wasn't even in his range of vision. He played loud rockabilly on a boom box when he did repairs. He drank beer in the evenings and got into fights. His work area looked like a battlefield. He also recognized more readily than I did that there was almost fifty years difference in our ages. He had no intentions of trying to close this gap himself. It was up to me.

I had three options: Find a new mechanic, sell the farm, or learn to communicate with young Luke. I chose the latter. There was a possible fourth option—to attempt my own repairs—but I did not allow for this.

I had to learn to speak to Luke. It did not begin well. My tractor broke down two days after I had found Luke brooding in the parts bins. It snarled, choked asthmatically, went bang, and died right in the middle of a field of grass. I went to our house and spent some time on the couch, looking out the window. Suzanne and Sheba the dog gave me wide berth. Finally, I gathered my resolve, went out to the tractor and stood staring at it. I considered fetching my toolbox. It was a helpless, fretful feeling. I went back into the house, knowing what I had to do.

Luke didn't answer the phone right away. When he finally did, after a half-dozen rings, he sounded more like a badger than a mechanic, but he agreed to come out to the farm. I waited a week for him to appear, my tractor perched forlornly under a tarp in the field as the grass grew around it. Finally, I dialed Luke's number again and held the phone away from my ear, but he didn't answer.

September 11, 2001, happened in the meantime. For a while I did not care if the grass grew over my head. Finally, a week later, I was able to tear myself away from anguish and drive to the shop in town. The bell on the door rang as I walked in, but no one came to the counter. I could hear loud country rock from the workroom in back. Luke wasn't listening to the news. I pulled the hinged gate up on the counter and walked through. Luke looked up from the motor he was repairing. Then he put his head back down. He said something, but I could not hear him.

"What?" I said.

He did not turn the music down. "I'll be out tomorrow after supper," he shouted. There was a deep cut over his eye, and his face was red.

I drove home in despair, listening on the car radio to the agonized reports from the Trade Towers scene. It was disorienting to be out on the road; it even seemed fearful to be traveling in gentle, bucolic Crawford County. The newspeople, who normally act as if they know all the answers, seemed distracted and frightened. Everything large and small in the world seemed askew. As I came over the rise to our house I saw my Bolens broken down in the field, but now it seemed like an annoying fly. Whatever difficulties I had were absorbed by the world's greater troubles. But like everyone else, I had to go on with things. It was the best thing to do.

Luke came the next day. He got out of his pickup, put his head under my tractor hood, and did some things. Then he slammed the hood down, turned the key switch, and the tractor ran again. I felt almost guilty to feel so relieved.

"What do I owe you?" I asked.

"A bottle of beer," Luke said.

"I'll do better than that," I said, surprised and pleased that he had made this congenial sign. "But come on, let's go up on the deck."

I opened two Leinenkugel lagers, and we sat together gazing down into the farm valley below, wondering what to say to each other. Luke guzzled his beer greedily, and I got him another.

"Tough times," he said finally.

"I can't remember feeling worse about things."

"The bastards!" His anger was quick-rising and genuine. He stood up, and I thought he was going to heave his bottle down into the brush on the hillside. He began pacing the deck.

"Luke, take it easy. Sit down," I presumed to say.

His eyes flared when he looked at me, but then he sat back down in the deck chair. "Did you see those buildings going down?" he said. "I never thought I'd see anything like that in my life. The filthy sons of bitches! Somebody's got to pay."

"We don't even know for sure who's responsible."

"When we find out, I want a crack at them."

His hands trembled as he picked at the label on his bottle. I tried to get his mind onto something else. "Are you staying busy?"

"Oh, I'm keeping up. But I'm going to have to hire some help pretty soon. Dad knew a lot of things. I miss him." I could see his sorrow rising over his anger now and knew he would not want to grieve in front of me.

"Of course you do. We all do."

"I wish I'd paid better attention. He could fix anything." Luke took another pull on his beer and steadied himself.

"If we get into a war and this thing goes on," he said, "I'm thinking I might close the shop down and join up. I'd like to get into the airborne." Luke is a very young man, but when he said this, even in the sunlight, his face grew shadowed and aged.

"That's mighty tough duty."

"Dad was in the marines in Vietnam," Luke said.

I had not known this. Gentle Ted.

"I never thought much beyond this town. But if there's a fight, I want to be in it."

"What will I do if my Bolens breaks down?" I was trying to tease him, see if I could get him to ease up and banter with me.

Luke peered at me carefully. "You could go write a poem," he said, and stopped me in my tracks. He wasn't smiling, he was giving me the old Magnuson straight face routine.

How did he know I was a poet? Ted! But how had Ted known?

"Dad told me you like ghost music, too." Then he gave me one of his unrestrained laughs.

"It's not fair. You know *all* my secrets."

"I'll bet dad told you a few of mine, too."

"No. He never did. We had our own business."

Luke's cheeks were flexing as he looked off at the silos on the ridge across the valley. "I don't know what dad would have wanted me to do. But I can't just stay around here turning wrenches if there's trouble."

Well, we "won" our war quickly with shock and awe. We are still surrounded by adversaries old and new, covert and outright, but so far Luke has not gone off to join the paratroopers.

He has an answering machine on his shop phone now, but he does not return messages. If I stop by, he waves to me congenially from under a tractor and says some words, which I cannot hear over the bombinating rockabilly. He has written up a work order for me. He will come eventually, but I must take my turn, and my needs are generally more urgent than his availability.

So I am learning to prostrate my sixty-nine-year-old body. My back and knees and arms are serious liabilities, but I am learning. It is late, but not too late. I go down on my own cold, oil-stained cement, down where everything hurts; a Schubert lieder romps elegantly from the cheap, little stereo on the steel shelf beside the cluttered work bench as I utter the vile words that men speak to cold, indifferent machines.

Last week I changed the oil in the Bolens. In describing this process, I will attempt to display the skills I acquired at National Automotive Services all those years ago: Changing the oil on the Bolens requires an almost hopeless, heartbreaking maneuver, performed while one is lying on a sore shoulder on a cold floor. With your free arm you reach around the hydraulic lift arms, over the drive shaft to the small oil plug, which is remotely located in dark obscurity between the engine and the mower deck. It is easiest if you can shape your forearm like a Z.

Only the smallest crescent wrench can be maneuvered into this limited space to eventually, and with considerable difficulty, be fitted over the plug head. When this is accomplished, there is perhaps a half-inch of space in which to turn the wrench before it has to be laboriously reset on the plug. All this must be accomplished by touch alone, because your aching arm, reaching into the machine, obscures any view.

I was in the midst of this agony when I suddenly realized that I had not remembered to set the foot brake on the tractor. If the tractor rolled by accident, my arm would have been pinched between the motor and the deck. My only option then would have been to call forlornly for Suzanne, who was far away in the house and would not know how to extract me if she did come.

And so, joint by painful joint, I struggled to my feet and wavered around the tractor until I could stand straight. I climbed up on the seat and pushed the brake down with my left foot while reaching down to set the holding lever with my hand. This lever sets into a groove and is held in place by a strong spring. I eased the lever into its notch and started to let up on the pedal—but the lever snapped up from its groove and the pedal gave me a resounding whack on my shin. My shoulders and the top of my head froze with shock as the pain arced up my leg.

I have a blood condition, a shortage of clotting agents that sometimes causes deep discoloration and bleeding dangers. I was going to have a midnight-colored bruise all the way up my leg, and I hoped the skin had not been broken.

Besides, it hurt. My God, it hurt like hell! I struggled off the tractor and began pacing back and forth on the gritty concrete. I heard a sound, beginning like a pennywhistle, descending abruptly to a growl, trailing off into a wail, then breaking into sobs. Over and over.

I realized, it was me. I was howling. Oh. And it hurt. It was me. Over and over.

Threnody

Wanda the Great Dane was dying. Beside me, her eyes were open and she still felt warm, but her breathing was uneven. I stroked her smooth fur and spoke to her, but she did not respond. We were in the bed of my pickup truck in a parking lot outside a veterinary hospital. Around us birds were fussing, people were talking in the distance, a train thrummed, a car horn blared, creatures were getting on with their lives, but Wanda was turning to silence. I tried to start a song with her, for she loved to sing more than most things, but she had no songs left. Her marvelous dark blue aura was already fading. There was nothing to do but take her in my arms and press my brow to her forehead as she grew cold. I tried to look into her eyes, to somehow reach into her depths and draw her back, but she was slipping away even as I held her.

She had been struck by a mysterious malady and was suddenly downed, her legs no longer able to support her. We had taken her to all the local veterinarians. No one could help.

I was desolate, yet angry, too. It seemed almost a cheat. Big dogs are vulnerable, but Wanda was a perfect friend. A loved dog should not be taken so suddenly. A good dog should not die.

Nor should a good father. I thought of this as I held Wanda in the truck bed. Seventeen years before at my father's funeral someone tried to console me by saying that there are things worse than death. Yes, one of them is living with irretrievable loss.

I was numb and diminished. Two days after my father's death, driving to his funeral, I reached into the back seat of the car impulsively to straighten my old gray suit on a hanger, and was suddenly plunging down the freeway midsection. By the time I was able to stop, I had broken an axle. I rented another car and went on.

My father had fallen in his little room and three days later died of the consequences. In the church again with a coffin, my mother dead four months before, I was an orphan now—an adult at last.

As I lay in the bed of my pickup, holding Wanda, I had another memory of my father, plugged with tubes, surrounded by blinking machines as he lay dying, heaving against his bonds, and storming against equivocation. The doctor and nurses asked him to be calm.

It is unnatural, not wanting to live anymore. It is hard, irregular work. The next day I sat with him as he strove mightily to dowse the last sparks in his body. I was hoping he would soon have his way. It is an aberrant thing, too, to hope your father will die.

As he rocked his head back and forth, he seemed puzzled. His hands were contracting, eyes flickering, lips trying to form words around the tubes that ran down his throat. Then in an instant, something deserted his body and he was no longer there, no longer my father, but a residue of my father growing cold. Not a life anymore, but a memory of life.

Eighty-two years. It had been a good run, but it was not enough. A good father should not die.

A few days before, I had been sitting with him in the intensive care room as he drifted in and out of consciousness. I remembered how, as a child, I pretended I was guarding him as he napped after an exhausting day at the circus.

He awakened with a snap, lifted his head and, when he saw me, tried in vain to speak. And so I spoke to him. I told him that I loved him. He looked away embarrassed, as he had always done, a man of his time and age. Then he struggled to turn his bound wrist and point at his back. His poor, curved spine. I knew he was in agony, having to lie flat on his back. I had asked the nurses if he could be turned on his side, but it was not possible. There was no more comfort to give.

"Dad," I said. "Blink once for no, two for yes. When you try to speak, are you saying that you want to die?" He blinked his eyes twice and looked away from me. This was an even harder thing to say than love, but he looked at me once more and blinked twice. Then he blinked twice again, this time perhaps for love.

Part Five ~

I struggle hard for life. I take physick, and take air;
my friend's chariot is always ready. We have run
this morning twenty-four miles, and could run
forty-eight more. But who can run the race with death?
—Doctor Samuel Johnson, from a letter

Real Words

It has always been real words that make most sense to me. If I have a soul, it is comprised of real words. Other things sometimes puzzle or daunt me, but real words have saved my life and spirit more times than I care to admit. Yes, they are my trouble, my frustration and failure; but if I am patient and respectful, they are my salvation. This is what matters most.

I do not utter real words in conversations, at dinner tables, or in meeting rooms, nor do I write them in memos, postcards, e-mail. My real words occur in solitude and time, and I write and speak them for myself.

When I was young, words were the only thing I could do well. I had no head for science and arithmetic, lacked concentration for history and catechism, did not have the ability to excel in sports. Words carried me through my various crises. If I felt threatened, words made some sense of things. I could count on them at least. Now, as I engage my senescence, once again in this last development of my life, real words are my faithful tools and best hope.

Perhaps I was not paying enough attention or in some state of denial, but in a wink, age was on me like a blitzkrieg. I was graying, then gray. My skin loosened, sagged, and fell to wrinkles. My eyes grew dry and small in their sockets. Minute X's and O's of red began to intersect on my nose and cheeks. My back hurt most of the time; other hints and minor maladies appeared and disappeared. I tried to stay busy—but it is unnerving when people start to raise their voices when they look at you, to make certain you hear what they have to say.

Mostly people do not see me now. I could strip and walk through fire, could go out ambling in a purple jump suit with an armadillo on a ribbon leash, and I would only get a glance or two. There is no sense trifling with delusions: hair dye, tummy tucks, rowing machines, cheery articles in *Modern Maturity*. I cannot overcome this development. I am out of focus, on my way to being invisible. If I resist this I become a hacked-off, disgruntled fool. If I give in to it, I become a slug on the wall.

But there are the words—the real words. I must remember what they mean, the patience they require, in my own time and silence, the sublime gift of their proportion and lucidity.

Suddenly, without any prelude or direct sense of cause and effect, I become ill. Doctors drill my bones and scan my innards like a poem. They draw my blood, and draw it again, counting and recounting its elements. All my apertures are probed and tested. The massive bruises on my shins and thighs are ominous. I am rolled into buzzing, muttering machines—a loneliness I do not like to remember—that scope my skull and skeleton. I am plugged, bent, siphoned, magnetized, radiated; I am advised that ultimately I might have to be deprived of some of my parts.

My condition is diagnosed as ITP—Idiopathic Thrombocytopenic Purpura. When the doctor first says these frigid, enormous words to me they seem to come as a hiss and growl. I cry, "Mercy!" He explains that it is a diminishment of platelets, the clotting agent in my blood. Something is wiping them out, perhaps a virus or some insidious disorder of my spleen. There is no known reason why this condition suddenly prevails, but we have to persuade whatever is attacking the platelets to desist. There is danger of serious internal and external bleeding.

I am transfused intravenously with gamma globulin, then given massive, extended doses of powerful steroids. The drugs push me toward indifference, send me drifting in the direction of some cold center I had been unaware of in myself. I reside in white, humming noise. My sleep is fitful, inflicted with strange, sometimes menacing dreams where I wander endlessly in caves of ice. The platelet count creeps up, but medicine tempers my sensibilities and numbs my psyche. I lurch through clinics and hospital rooms, roam large, antiseptic buildings, joining the parade of ill, worried people shuffling from waiting room to waiting room.

But still I compel myself, keep my mind and eye on the words. My pencil moves on paper, and I seek real words. I keep scribbling even under the steady drips of IVs, the benumbing, yet jangling doses of steroids, between ministrations of doctors and nurses. The real words are my anchor against the withdrawal that beckons so seductively.

After all my years of being resolutely connected, it is difficult to explain or describe this threatening detachment. Only a metaphor can serve. I am in an automobile entering a turnpike on a winter night, gearing down for a tollbooth as snow twills through my headlight beams. Paper cups and wrappers scramble in frigid wind on the ice and spattered oil. No unsmiling, emptied face is at the booth window—instead I push a button, a machine snarls and sticks out my ticket like a yellow tongue, receiving me into an unwelcoming, cold hell.

I shift from first to second gear as I turn the curve of the ramp, then into third at the top, craning my neck to look left as I enter the lane, shove the gear down to fourth, then up to fifth and set the cruise control.

The highway looms beyond my headlights like a blank page or a waiting room. Illuminated signs and prefabricated warehouses disguise the roadside. The broken centerline slips into my eyes, passing out my ears to stream from the back of my head.

I am adrift on ice and asphalt; empty cans, shattered safety glass, potholes, and rugs of animals pasted to my lane. At this moment I cannot imagine that another human being might be thinking of me. Warmth and humanity have nothing to do with this passage. It is a mindless time to be lived alone, the steady whir of tires, snow coiling down to the windshield, wipers sweeping it away—a drab, exhausted story to be told only to myself, to be endured more than experienced, teaching me how to forget and be forgotten. The night grows more measureless and obscure. It seems that I am on a journey toward evanescence, taking a thousand or ten thousand miles to unravel, the dispassionate narrative droning on invariably through its tepid beginning and middle, toward what I imagine might be its cheerless end.

Idiopathic Thrombocytopenic Purpura. My friend, Jim McKean, an avid fisherman, comments, "Oh man, that name sounds like one of the flies that a fly-fisherman ties using imported feathers, fur, and #8 thread—and a barbed hook."

The turnpike metaphor goes on, but now it is the metaphor of choice and imagination. I am daunted by the winter night, but take an exit, pay my fare, and drive out of the swirling snow into a pristine, starry countryside. I do not know where I am, but stop, switch off, open the door, and stand in splendor.

I tick like the motor as silence presses in; but silhouettes of trees are buoyant above the drifts. Beyond the road, snow-tufted skeletons of wild carrots and goldenrod poke above the drifted fields and barbed wire fences. There are farm lights in the distance; a dog barks and moans with cold.

There is no moon, only the slow, dimensionless turn of stars. Then light begins rising in the east, casting across the drifts, showing the intricate feathers of ice on the snow crust as if they are crystal moths. The dark bruises of disease and aging begin to fade as dawn strokes the horizon, and I become a particle of brightness.

The real words, their promise and redemption, had helped bear me through. Now there is the rest of my life to live. Many difficult things have passed; much has been given and much taken away. But somehow I am sound again and, for the moment, without misgivings.

I wish I did not have to think that I endured this crisis—the ordeal, the journey through snow—in order to gain new resolution. But perhaps I was being "taught" something. Hard lessons, we called them when we were younger—the things that prepared us for the difficulties of life. Now I am being prepared for the difficulties of death.

The challenges are mortal now. They will come again. There is still joy, pleasure, even some wonder, but also a consistent sense of exigency. Yet, I have this quiet room, pencil and paper, and my resolute desire for words, the real words that sustain me.

Big Joe Turner

I lurch from a hot soak in the bathtub into the kitchen and see my doughnut cushion on a chair. Improbably, I have this vision of Big Joe Turner and sit down on the cushion, beginning a loud, awkward chorus of "The Midnight Special." Suzanne looks at me as if I have finally turned in my keys.

I have never spent much time thinking about Joe Turner. For fifty years his voice has growled and tolled to me, lingering for a long time even when the music has stopped, teaching me courage and endurance. But now as I sing, I am thinking of him.

I was in the same room with Turner only once, in the early 1980s, a few years before he died. In New York on book publishing business, I was looking for an evening out. I scoped the *Times* to see who was in town and discovered that he was appearing in a small neighborhood club. After an early dinner, I caught a cab, paid the cover, and got a table by myself.

The musicians had already arrived and were stoking up at the bar before the first set. On the stand there was a piano, guitar, drums, bass, and a tenor sax put down on a chair. Near the microphone was a sturdy padded stool—and there was a doughnut cushion placed in the middle of it.

Eventually the piano player came to the set and played some blues, then the other musicians drifted on to join him, working for fifteen minutes to warm themselves up and get the audience ready.

Then the pianist stepped to the microphone and said, "Everybody's waitin' for you, great man. Where are you?"

A big voice from the bar in the next room bawled, "Man, you *know* where I am!"

"Well get in here. People lookin' for you."

"I'm comin', just gimme a minute!" The pianist sat down again at the keyboard and the group hit a light blues tempo.

Finally a huge figure shambled into view, hair ironed and slicked back, three-hundred-plus lumpy pounds, sliding along on carpet slippers and bearing down on his cane. He was working hard, shifting all his painful gears like an overloaded train, but still it took him a long time to get to the stool as the rhythm waited for him. He eased down on his doughnut cushion and—before anyone knew it was happening—he slipped into "The Honeydripper," his big voice making me tingle and grin. Then, one after another—"Flip, Flop and Fly," "Honey Hush," "Cherry Red," "Good Mornin' Blues," "Stoop Down Baby"— he had them all down cold, not quite as snappy and fresh as in the old days when he was a legendary, indestructible giant, scuffling and bouncing drunks out of bars, but he still delivered the tunes with plenty of mustard on them.

Joe Turner was born to sing the blues. I cannot imagine anyone suggesting that he could have done anything else with his life. He *knew* he was doing something important, and his voice resounded out of the night with ease and authority—a rough shouter, but capable also of tender, exuberant lyricism, as long as the music leaned toward the blues. The songs were of sadness, betrayal, love, loss, and endless erotic endurance. The blues didn't spare Joe Turner his suffering, but maybe when he sang he was holding time back.

I was not born to sing the blues—but I sit on my doughnut cushion with my head thrown back and croak:

> My sister wrote a letter, my mother wrote a card—
> "If you want to come an' see us, you'll have to ride the rods."
>
> Let the Midnight Special shine its light on me,
> Let the Midnight Special shine its ever-lovin' light on me.

Hell, it is so beautiful! It makes me feel good. All I need is a rhythm section. If I can just do it right I will be cured of all maladies. At least while I am singing, I will not be growing older.

Infections

O Rose thou art sick.
—William Blake

I am thinking about Scobey when I read in the newspaper about the deer herd being attacked by helicopters in the state park. Scobey told me once that he likes to hunt. He said he didn't care whether he got his deer; he just loved to walk in the woods with his gun as his dad had taught him. He was standing beside the shelves of canned vegetables in his doomed store when he said this. His big red jaws got redder and he took his rimless glasses off to rub his tired eyes. "Sometimes I'd see 'em, but I wouldn't even take my safety off." Scobey is thirty now, going on sixty. All he does is work. He hasn't had time to go hunting in half a dozen years.

Eighteen deer near our area recently tested positive for Chronic Wasting Disease. The Department of Natural Resources has set up a 361 square-mile "eradication zone," extending into three counties of southwestern Wisconsin where they intend to wipe out the whole herd of twenty-five-thousand. I am not sure of how they will dispose of the carcasses. Two plans have been mentioned: Either they will incinerate them all or dump the bloodied bodies into a huge landfill. Perhaps both. Twenty-five thousand dead deer. The mind falls away from such things. The plan seems like something dreamed up by a war council. The DNR started the other morning at dawn by killing a sample group for further testing. They swooped in with choppers over the evacuated park and gunners picked off anything that looked like a deer.

CWD is a deadly brain infection similar to mad cow disease. The Department of Natural Resources seems confused and daunted. The

151

New York Times quotes a Wisconsin DNR official as saying, "I think everybody has some doubts. This is uncharted territory." The infection is caused by a protein particle called a prion. I looked up "prion" in my unabridged dictionary: "Any of several petrels of the southern hemisphere . . . that somewhat resemble doves." This makes me feel even more uncertain about what is going on. But my unabridged is dated 1981, so I look up "prion" in my word processor dictionary: "A microscopic particle similar to a virus but lacking nucleic acid, thought to be an infectious agent responsible for scrapie and certain other degenerative diseases of the nervous system." No mention of the petrels. But a lot of southwestern Wisconsin people are worrying about how CWD will affect hunting season.

At least half a dozen deer browse and live on our 117 acres of fields and woods. I'd like to know if they are going to have to die and certainly I want to know why.

Soldiers Grove is a little town of not more than five hundred people, most of them over forty years old. There is a small motel, pharmacy, a bed and breakfast inn, a senior citizen home, a couple of taverns, a small public library, a hair stylist, a car repair garage, and a land excavator. Except in hunting season, there aren't enough folks living in the area to really make things prosper.

When Scobey took over the grocery store, he was twenty-four, just a big, blond baby boy a few years out of high school; a grocery wunderkind, he had already been clerking and bagging for a decade in the area. The store was on its last legs, a worn-out, indifferent place; but Scobey scrubbed it up, posted bright new signs, put in a new deli counter, and even stocked some fan belts and fishing lures. There was a case of fresh cheese curds at the cash register and a few VCRs to rent. When you came to his store, Scobey took the time to say hello and chat a bit. They interviewed him for the *Crawford County Independent* when he started up and he said, "I guess I was born to be a grocery man. My dad taught me a lot. He died young, but he was a grocery man."

In this lush, early summer, I am happy to be out, ambling in urgent meadows and under the new canopies of trees. I am happy to be well again. I can't remember much about last summer—my Idiopathic Thrombocytopenic Pupura summer—except being infected, lying on the couch in our library, and gazing numbly for hours at the sunlit dirt road curving up to the old pump on the rise. I could see my writing shack in the distance, but my legs weren't working right, and I could not shuffle up the road to do any work. But sometimes I scribbled a few words on a pad beside the couch.

Last summer I did not care much about anything. Time began to swallow itself. But I looked forward each day to the regular appearance of the six young deer in the south meadow in the late afternoons, ambling and browsing, strong and young, lifting their heads suddenly to small alerts, then passing slowly across the road on their way up to the tall grass meadows on the far ridge where they would bed down for the night.

They took their time as they moved. Though I was abstracted and remote, their leisurely passage made me feel that I was still connected to the earth. I cherished their healthy alertness. Even Sheba our dog held off barking and watched with me, seeming to enjoy their predictability.

The infection of my blood exhausted me and the prescribed medicine neutralized my body and spirit. When I walked I wanted to stop, when I stopped I wanted to lie down, when I was down I wanted to nap, when I napped I had terrible dreams that woke me up, and so I tried to walk again. But mostly I lay still on the couch. The days reached into each other, extending on and on with summer brightness, but I could not bring myself to care. Clocks ticked in other rooms, but not in the one where I was lying. But that was last summer. This summer I am walking, talking, writing, rousing the deer in the meadows, toiling in our garden, mowing the lawn, running errands into Soldiers Grove.

Things went along okay for Scobey and his store, but then they built a Super Wal-Mart in Viroqua, only a twenty-minute drive away. The community started bussing folks from the senior citizens home down the road to the Wal-Mart, delivering them with their social security checks to drift in the cavernous aisles of the mega-store.

A few months later a gasoline One Stop was built right across the road from Scobey's, and they sold milk, butter, cheese, bread, eggs, doughnuts, beer, candy, soft drinks, bottled water, and snacks to the people who bought gas. Sometimes Scobey forgot to shave his big, red cheeks, and his eyes started to sag behind his unwiped, rimless spectacles. But he kept his sleeves rolled up, kept stocking his skimpy shelves and cutting meat on his block.

I am working at the table in my writing shack up on the ridge in this summer of wellness. Sheba the dog hears it first and lifts her head. Someone is coming in on the long dirt road. I get up and look out the window. It is Richie Halverson on his motor scooter. Whenever Richie needs to talk to me about something serious he comes to my shack in the morning, because he knows that's where I'll be.

He sets his kickstand, shuffles up, and knocks gently as he peers in the door window. I can tell he is bothered about something.

"Hey, Richie," I say. "Come on in."

Richie is an articulate and discursive farmer monologist. He starts slowly and politely. I know it will take him a while to get to what is really on his mind.

"Say, Paul, how's it going? You got bluebirds in that house out there on the tree. You know that? Some rain wouldn't hurt us, you know. The corn's starting to bite in. What about that deer disease? Do you suppose they're going to have to shoot 'em all? How could that be?" He looks out my window at some passing shreds of clouds, then jerks his head and goes on. "Well, them Cubs are learning new ways to lose. Say, did you know that Scobey is closing down his store?" Richie brings the news. I did not know about the store closing, but now I am thinking about Scobey as Richie goes on with his country litany: tales of grasshoppers, his neighbor's shed roof, rabbits eating his wife's lettuce, shooting stars, firewood, tractor troubles, church bazaars.

Sheba is sniffing Richie's trouser cuffs. Finally he pauses and reaches down to stroke her neck.

"Hello, girl," he says. Richie thinks I coddle Sheba—and he is right. "You like that old cow manure, girl?"

He gives me a shy, quick glance, then looks away. I know it is time for him to tell me what is bothering him. "Say, Paul," he says. "I wanted to tell you. I'm missing more than a dozen heifers. I can't tell what happened. A tree fell over the fence down by Pine Knob Road and they might of got out there and gone across into the woods. I haven't had time to look good, but I wanted you to know, in case you see something. They're just gone," he said in wonder.

I've lived most of my life in cities and towns. When something is missing I think the worst thing first. "Richie, do you suppose you've been rustled?"

Richie has lived all his life near Soldiers Grove. "I don't think so. I just need 'em back. I can't take a loss like that. How the hell could you steal a dozen heifers anyway?"

But I can tell he is thinking about this. He shakes his head. "What kind of cowboys we got around here who would do something like that?"

"Same kind of guys who break into the summer cabins along the river. Maybe this time they figured they'd try for something big. You ought to call the sheriff."

"I think I'll wait a while before doing that. I'll see what I turn up. They're probably off in the trees on one of my far forties."

"Can I give you a hand?" I ask. Richie is a cordial man, but he knows I would just be in the way.

"Naw, no thanks, Paul. I'd just appreciate it if you'd keep your eyes open. There's a lot of space here. They're gonna turn up."

Scobey was born to be a softball player, too, but he rarely has a chance to prove it. I once watched him play in a slow pitch tournament under the lights at the Dairy Days celebration in Soldiers Grove. It was the first year he owned the store and he bought white T-shirts for his buddies that said "Scobey's" in big red letters and he got red matching caps for them. He was very proud. He played first base, blinking behind his big glasses when he batted, but he had marvelous reflexes and a hitter's powerful stride. When he connected, the ball sailed a long way over the snow fence that marked the outfield, across some old railroad tracks, into the darkened fields beyond. They couldn't find the balls he hit into the tall grass and sumac. He hit three home runs in the game I watched and he was having fun. Later his team lost out in the tournament to a team sponsored by a Quik Stop in Boscobel, even though Scobey hit two more dingers.

After this, he didn't have time for softball. He couldn't afford T-shirts and he couldn't afford fulltime clerks in the store, so his mom helped him, and Scobey worked at least twelve to fifteen hours *every* day.

We are shopping for a few items at Scobey's and buy a copy of a Wisconsin newspaper.

An article reads, "The DNR said its goal was to try to kill nearly 25,000 deer in the 361 square-mile zone as quickly as possible in hopes of stopping the disease. But now the DNR said it doesn't expect many deer—probably only 500—to be killed during the summer, which means the bulk will have to be shot in the fall." The plan means that in the autumn one deer will be killed in the zone for every ten acres. If the zone is extended into our area, at least a dozen deer might be shot dead on my property. I have no idea what would happen to their carcasses. Will trucks come in to haul them away to the gory landfill? I do not easily envision such carnage.

There are other articles about the world's infections: suicide bombings, border skirmishes, preparations for war, terrorist plotting, more accusations against Catholic priests.

Richie's lost heifers finally turn up, four days later. Driving around the countryside in his pickup, worried and worn-out, Richie spots them in a distant meadow, off a private dirt road running past a wounded, overgrown farm owned by two ne'er-do-well brothers who inherited it from their parents. The brothers spend most of their time letting the place fall apart around them. When Richie knocks on the door to inquire, he is told to fuck off.

Richie finally goes to the sheriff and they use binoculars to identify his cows from the road. The brothers resist violently and have to be restrained when the sheriff and his deputies come in with a warrant. There's a big stash of marijuana in two closets and more growing in their far fields.

The brothers were coming home from a tavern late one night and found Richie's cows out. They herded them up the road to their place in the middle of the night and ran them into a remote field on their land. They needed some quick money and intended to sell them to some fly-by-night cattle dealer.

Richie is undone. "This used to be a nice place to live," he says sadly. "What kind of guys would do something like that? You should have seen 'em. They were so far gone they looked like goats with the mange, and smelled worse. One of 'em bit a deputy. I got so upset when it was over I headed down to Scobey's to buy a six-pack, and then I remembered Scobey is closed. What are we coming to here? We don't need this."

When Scobey finally decided to close his store, he did it right, posting notices to the community as he phased out. No one really believed that he was going to stop. It seemed like the store had always been there for our small needs. But Scobey knew what he had to do.

He was going to have to file for bankruptcy. When he locked his doors for good, he got down with his big raw bones and spent two weeks cleaning the place up. Scobey works. That is what he does. He toils impossible hours everyday, even when he is out of business.

The summer after my infected summer, Suzanne and I plant a patch of tomatoes and peppers. We have never fully assimilated the process of gardening. We want to grow gorgeous, delectable things, but don't always follow through with all the necessary steps. We lack finesse, but we are usually earnest.

It is a dry summer and things begin to parch. The garden is set off at a distance from the house, so I accumulate many gallon milk jugs and line them up in our wheelbarrow. Every evening as the sun goes down, while Suzanne is cooking dinner, I fill the jugs at the spigot beside the house and roll my load through the heat to the garden where I tenderly dampen the powdery earth around our plants. Over the weeks I grow to dread this hot, heavy task, but I persist like Jean de Florette to bear water to my plants.

Through all my sweaty scuffling, I envision our plump tomatoes cool and sliced, dusted with French pepper on my plate. They swell larger, then one day begin to stripe yellow—and then turn bright red and mellow in the sun. I decide to let them ripen just a few more days on the vine.

Next day I struggle out to the garden with my head down and my wheelbarrow full of sloshing jugs. I look up at my rewards. They are all gashed open and sickened, pulpy and ruined, their juice dripping into the dirt. All of them.

Then I see my enemies gnawing insidiously on the fruits, like bright green octopus tentacles sucking on each globe. One can almost hear their grinding—tobacco leaf hornworms, some bigger than my fingers, swollen fat with moisture, the water I have laboriously borne all summer.

I reel with loathing, gather myself, and wade into the vines, tearing these infections off my fruits, dashing them to the earth, where they writhe and bleed green. But it is hopeless, and I am soon exhausted, stagger to the house to give Suzanne the bad news.

A few weeks ago I had to go to the Wal-Mart to buy some garden hose and walked through their grocery department. There was Scobey stocking bins. Of course he had his sleeves rolled up and was bearing down on his work. When he looked up and saw my stricken face, he took his glasses off to wipe them with his handkerchief.

"Hello, Mr. Zimmer," he said. He put his glasses back on and placed a comforting hand on my back. "It's okay. I'm a grocery man. These folks are lucky to have me."

Fleeing War

It is late February 2002, and we are preparing for a trip to France. Our original airline tickets were dated September 12, 2001. In the last months Suzanne and I have cancelled new reservations three times. Warnings and rumors of evildoing are ubiquitous now, and some days are worse than others. Our losses are already unthinkable. Our leaders stand resolute in front of television cameras, but caught in off moments they appear to be vexed and human. Only glib commentators and retired generals act as if they know the real news and purport to have firm opinions. But the future is indeterminate, and this time it is different. Our enemies are murderous shadows and we do not know where they lurk. We are unaccustomed to the disquiet we feel in our lives, yet without being foolhardy, we must continue to move with care in such a world.

I stand ankle deep in the snow on our ridge in southwestern Wisconsin and gaze down at the frozen river twisting through the valley toward Soldiers Grove. Cold wind fingers my scarf and creeps up under my stocking cap. In the distance below I see the tiny figures of a rabbit hunter and his dog poking in the brushy woods that fill the draws. Clouds are mounting and the afternoon is growing dark. More snow is on the way. In the south of France it is almost early spring.

Pensively, we have set our reservations again. As we make these arrangements, we think of France and our small eighteenth-century house. High up on the stones, just under its eaves out of the weather, is a crude drawing of a battle in Napoleon's aborted Egyptian campaign, made by a campaigner who managed to return. There are representations and signs of endless, old wars everywhere in France. It reminds you of how French people for centuries had to press on with their days, not knowing what might come next. The same has been true of American generations that lived through the half dozen wars we fought just in the twentieth century. We feel anxiety knotting again in our bodies and souls—not so much fear for our lives, but a dread of further disorder, a lack of control, and deep concern for young people going off to war.

Recalling my own youth and military conscription, the days when I believed, as did Joseph Conrad's character in *Youth*, "that I could last forever," I begin to worry about my gentle teenage grandson and the prospect of a military draft. The days of harsh news make me feel aged and vulnerable.

I try to express my concern to my son. This is not something he likes to think about; he is in his late thirties and enjoying his prime, but I ask him to consider ways of preparing my grandson so that he might, if necessary, show proof of his beliefs as a pacifist. Perhaps he could join the Quaker church or work with other organized peace groups. I did not have this opportunity when I was young. When and where I came from there was no substitute for "doing your duty," and we admired only one kind of bravery. Being brave about your convictions was not an acceptable alternative.

At the induction center when I was drafted, they herded hundreds of us, naked except for our shoes, through the various stages of the physical examination. We were not beautiful, undraped youth, but a spectacle of absurd chattel. At one point we were told to line up, bend over and spread the cheeks of our buttocks so that a doctor could peer into our anuses with a flashlight. As he walked down the row, pausing to peer into our dark interiors, one man, perhaps by accident, loudly broke wind. The doctor, already appalled by what he had to do, stood back and viciously kicked the man sprawling across the room, where he struck his head against a radiator and crumpled bloody and unconscious. The doctor was still a doctor and, reluctantly remembering the oath of his profession, moved to treat him.

At the end of the physical, we were lined up in a large room under an American flag and told to repeat a vow of service to our country, agreeing to defend it with our lives. After reciting this, we were told to take a step forward, symbolizing our acceptance of the pledge. Allegedly, at this point we had a choice, but we were aware that the unstated alternative was arrest and shame. We had our clothes on again and felt less cold and lonely. All of us stepped forward as we were ordered, even the already wounded man.

Our secretary of defense warns us clearly that he expects America to be attacked again by terrorists and the results are "likely to be worse" than what we have already experienced. We are informed that a "shadow government" is in place, residing in secret underground bunkers so that government can proceed in the event of an "unthinkable" disaster in Washington. President Bush, grasping for harsh imagery, impoliticly harks back to the horrors of World War II, trying to indicate the seriousness of the threat, and declares that we must contend with an "axis of evil." He warns Iraq, Iran, and North Korea that we regard it a serious affront that they do not comply with weapons inspections. He cautions any other nation that harbors terrorists or produces weapons of mass destruction that we will consider them to be our enemy.

The Israelis and Palestinians continue to scourge each other, heightening the atmosphere of violence. We are regularly cautioned that there are umbrageous enemies in our midst, dedicated to destroying our lives. Some of them might be posing as our coworkers, drinking buddies, neighbors, or fellow passengers.

Once again Suzanne and I pack our bags for France. Preparing for these excursions has always been pleasant, but there is no whimsy or happy anticipation in our labors now. We have already packed and unpacked several times as we cancelled our reservations in the wake of highly threatening news. This time we are even more assiduous in our work, making certain not to include scissors, razors, pocketknives, or other sharp instruments in our luggage. We work with care in order not to appear suspicious to travel workers.

We are made paranoid by the media. We are told that our fellow passengers are potential enemies. A man's shoes could blow us out of the sky. A lethal blade could be inserted in the lining of a carry-on bag. Someone could have explosives strapped to their crotch. This is not magical realism; it is hysterical, sudden, unavoidable realism. It is like being kicked across a room by an angry doctor.

We have this modest house in a village in Languedoc, tucked into the lovely foothills of the Pyrenees, which, for one reason or another, we have not seen for three years. We have pined for it. Spring is coming. We believe it will console us to return to this place we love and regard as our second home, where for some years we have gone to dwell for brief periods as strangers in a friendly place. Now the world between Soldiers Grove, Wisconsin, and Puivert, France, seems alien to us—a shadowy, abstract world.

This is holy season in the Muslim world, a time of pilgrimage, and we watch on television multi-thousands of men swirling around the Kaaba in Mecca. They are focused and devout, unquestioning in their passionate belief. Their prayer is similar to the Lord's Prayer, but they do not beg forgiveness for trespasses or for deliverance from evil; they have come on their hajj to express their gratitude for the glory of Allah. They seem a kind of adorant force in their robes; not much changed since medieval times. One of the mullahs at the Kaaba leads prayers for the Muslims fighting in the jihads in Pakistan, Afghanistan, Kashmir, and Palestine.

Are these our enemies? If you compare them with the chic tourists and curious faithful in designer jeans and sunglasses, jammed into St. Peter's Square on Easter, it is hard to imagine a dialogue between these two worlds.

Forty years ago, when I was managing the UCLA campus bookstore, an Arabic exchange student took exception to our textbook buyback program. Our policy was to pay students half price for their books if they were still under class adoption and returned to us in good shape. This student would not accept that we were unable to give him back the full amount he had paid for his books. He returned again and again to the desk to challenge our policy, pacing and raging at me. My office phone rang and the clerk would announce, "He's here again." He accused me of taking advantage of exchange students. He railed against Americans and their abuses. I asked him what his country was.

"I am from what you call one of the 'underdeveloped nations.' I am from Pakistan. Do you know where that is?" I acted as if I did, but I was not certain.

One day finally, in total exasperation, he threw his books at me. "Here! Keep them, pig! If you must abuse me, if you cannot be fair with me, I do not want your capitalist American filth." He walked away, wiping his hands.

Suzanne and I zip shut our bags. We will set forth into this world from our tranquil, isolated home in Wisconsin. It will be, we believe, a relief to go to another quiet corner, to a country not our own. The last time we were there, the French were teasing us about President Clinton's indiscretions, but there is nothing to tease about now. We set forth on our journey in wariness, bearing a pervasive sadness.

After being away so long, we will smile and greet our friends and neighbors. We hope to settle in for a while, chat with them in our stuttering French, go to their shops and restaurants for their wonderful food and drink, ride their trains, stroll their ancient landscape, and perhaps break bread and have wine with a few of them.

The day before our departure the weather assaults us in Wisconsin with the first major blizzard of a mild winter. Eight inches of snow fall and it is still driving past our windows. I've been out three times shoveling a path clear to the car. Down the wooded hill we hear the snowplow struggling in the distance on County Highway C. It will be a while before they clear the two-mile dirt road that leads to our house. The Madison airport is a two-hour drive in good weather.

Primitive people have a better sense than we do of the nature of things. They would interpret this blizzard as a sign. We are too modernized for such quaint beliefs—nevertheless, we experience a kind of atavism. Suzanne has a lower abdominal pain, and as I look out the window at the snow I feel slightly dizzy.

The big orange snowplow makes it through. We wave from our window to smiling, massive Dave Pugh as he swings the truck past our library and turns to head back down the road, making wings of snow fly. Soon we will take a walk down the cleared road. Tomorrow morning we head out into this troubled world.

As we drive out in the morning, two gray foxes move through the snowy woods near our dirt road. They are a rare sight. They keep their wary eyes on us as they move slowly away. Solemn and beautiful in the sifting snow, they give us a good sign to begin our journey.

We arrive two hours early at the Madison airport. We are permeated with war and danger, tension reported by the media, looking for things to fear. We anticipate a major shakedown, but are whisked through security as if these were the Eisenhower years. One young man looks at me pointedly as I gaze around, but when I break eye contact with him and then look back, he has gone on to other things. We sit for a long time in the waiting area, reading war news in the New York Times, listening to people babble importantly on their cell phones.

What can be said about flying at thirty thousand feet in a huge airplane for seven hours? Light to dark to light, the constant drone, no sights to see, a dull book to read, an insipid movie to watch after a bland meal.

We pass swiftly and without particular scrutiny through European customs in DeGaulle airport, whisk our way across Paris in the Metro to the Gare Montparnasse, boarding a sleek TGV train which plunges us in a blur over the landscape of southern France in exactly five hours to Toulouse—not even time to dream of the old steam trains that once ran this route, taking all day and part of a night.

Numbed by speed and time, we obtain our rental car and drive to the Hotel du Commerce in Mirepoix. It is a relief to sense things slowing down. The hotel is very old and French, a black dog at the desk, shadowy hallways, uneven floors, hard beds, ancient hotel furniture, strange green lamps, and faded peach-colored wallpaper.

Already the war seems distant. Next morning, after shopping for groceries, we drive to Puivert and open our plain stone row house in the outskirts of the village. It is a great glory to be back, and the place is in excellent shape after three years. We gaze out the window of the balcony at the foothills of the Pyrenees and the beautiful valley with the Troubadour castle on a rise. Our neighbors wave to us. Bonjour!

Bonjour! The television in the house is not working and we cannot get the BBC on our short wave radio. The local store does not carry English language newspapers. We cannot understand the French newscasts. We are blessed with ignorance.

The next day we shop the small open-air market in nearby Chalabre and a woman selling olives asks if we are Anglais.

Non, non. Américain.

She looks at us with sympathy and asks if we are from New York.

No. Wees-cohn-son.

We pass a newsstand. *Le Figaro's* headlines read: "Contre L'Irak, Bush compte ses allies," and "Guerre totale au Proche-Orient."

There are splendid birds in the valley that sweep in for the breadcrumbs we put out on our balcony. Yellow-breasted great-tits, wagtails, black redstarts, early nightingales. Magpies even rush in to snatch morsels, dressed so urbanely, yet so brassy. A magnificent harrier skims the meadows. A shrike sits in a treetop behind the house across the street, bringing his prey back to his perch to pick apart, tossing fur and feathers off into the wind.

We drive the winding road up through the lush, spectacular Forêt du Picaussel to the Plateau du Sault, a sweeping high plain of grass and long, pure light with vistas of mountains in all directions. We turn toward Espezel and Belcaire, on to Ax la Thermes, driving through snow-covered mountains; the landscape shimmering, mountains looming white in front of even taller snow-covered peaks. The snow is just starting to melt in the sun. It is the beginning of spring, the first white tricklings. Skiers click past us in their plastic gear and snowshoes, pulling gleeful children on sleds. We stop and lunch in the car on pâté, Ariégeois cheese, bread, red wine, a few olives, and an apple.

Later we drive to Foix, park the car, and walk back up into the narrow, medieval streets to look at antique stores and old dwellings, then take a glass of beer in the sun at a cafe. When we get home there is a group of women talking to workmen renovating a house at the end of the row. Suzanne introduces us in halting French, explaining that we are the Americans who have the house two doors down. I watch the women as Suzanne tells them our nationality. They look at us with concern.

In the house we turn on the French Classique radio station. An hourly newscast comes on and Suzanne tries to understand the French. Finally she says, "Well, George Bush did something, but I can't tell you what."

Next morning long wisps of clouds extend over the mountains. Very quickly the soft pink becomes muted and lovely, growing subtle against the heightening blue. A magpie screams in a treetop, its whole body jerking forward as it yaks in agitation. But sun streams past the mountains now, and the mist becomes aureate. Clouds fill the notch over Campbrion. The aura grows silvery, then dims to a pale grayness that diminishes finally in the clear air.

We go to the market and, acquiescing to our anxieties, buy a *Herald-Tribune*. We put our groceries away, take the long walk around the valley, then sit down with the newspaper. The Pentagon announces its intention to build up a new arsenal of special atomic weapons that can "penetrate caves." There is an editorial about how Israel, surrounded by Muslims, will ultimately be overwhelmed. Arafat and Sharon taunt each other. Bin Laden has disappeared. There are firefights in Afghanistan and more American casualties. I start our evening fire with the newspaper.

We drive to Nebias and up on to the Plateau in a late afternoon. The air is bright, the vibrancy and tension of colors slips and changes as we drive—the whites and blues, yellows, greens, and browns. We park and begin to walk. The light across this high plain, so long and profound, sweeps around and passes through us as if we do not exist.

We go back into the Forêt and walk a rough path to the Maquis memorial, an evocation of their wooden hideout in the mountains, set in a cleared area where the resistors could receive Allied parachute drops of supplies and stash them in caves in the woods. There are copies of old photographs of these brave men and boys in display cases on the walls, and accounts in French of how they harassed the Nazis and interfered with their maneuvers, paying with their lives when they were caught.

The place is quiet, just birds fussing in the trees. We sign the guest register and note that the last visitors had come a week before us.

When we get back to our car there is a Frenchman playing with his dog on the road. He asks if we are afraid of *les chiens*. No, no. We pet his dog. He suggests that we take a hike up the hill on a rutted road that juts along the mountainside. We walk until we come to a break in the trees and an overwhelming vista—mountain upon mountain, sweeping up over and against each other, on and on, the colors and shapes beyond words, the blue sky and passing puffs of clouds. We stand for a long time together in silence. On our way back out we come upon a very deep cave, evoking a powerful contrast—the buoyant upsweep of the brilliant mountains, then the shadowy depth and dankness of the cave going straight down into the earth.

Walking to buy bread at the boulangerie in Chalabre a few days later, we see this headline in the newsstand: "Bush Puts His Finger on the Nuclear Button." We stop to scan the papers. Everyone is talking tough—Bush, Blair, Cheney, Rumsfeld, Hussein, the Al Queda leaders.

Arafat boasts how he has always been able to "out-trick" Sharon. The two old men bait each other as their people die under assault. There is little sign of sensitive, meaningful talk on the earth.

We meet a pleasant British couple at the next table in a restaurant in Limoux. Suzanne comments that we are grateful for Tony Blair's supportive remarks after September 11. The British woman comments, "Well, some of us wish that he would stop dabbling in world affairs now and take care of his business at home." It makes us feel lonely.

Driving to the Mediterranean shore, we pass old military fortifications near Collioure: big Napoleonic barracks and First and Second World War pillboxes that line the coast. Someone has sprayed words in sky blue paint on one of the pillboxes—"No More."

Collioure is radiant, with a famous lighthouse and bay painted by Derain, Matisse, Miró, Signac. We sit in the morning sun, having coffee in a seaside cafe and watch the shimmer on the water.

Four large khaki boats float into view through the serene water, rowed by French army recruits in camouflaged fatigues. Officers buzz around them in a motorized craft, bellowing orders through bullhorns. The French gaze at them, then turn away, apparently having grown used to them and their violation of this light painted by great artists.

We come out from our hotel at sunset to sit in a cafe and watch the bright ball settle into a bank of fog and clouds. It goes down quickly— just the top of it visible at last, two radiant eyes of light peeping momentarily out of streams of mist before it drops away. Things seem to slow down as it disappears—people, birds, light. A huge flock of gulls swirls over the illuminated clouds. Two beautiful young women in black pants suits, long, *black*, Spanish hair, walk proudly along the shore. People with baby carriages, families chatting, elderly couples in dark rich evening clothes.

The stripe of light grows dim and broadens as it ripples, and the clouds are still bright above it. Now people are wearing jackets as they walk in the cooler air off the water. A fishing boat appears in the breakwaters, like a half-fruit in the last light; one man is rowing as the other trolls. A jogger strides by in silhouette against the shining water. A young couple kisses in the twilight.

We return to Puivert and next morning as I cut fruit for breakfast I look out at oval clouds over the foothills, like large white dinner plates. A rooster in the yard behind the house shreds the air with his announcements. The French newscasters are talking about America. I don't know what they are saying. I try not to care, but I do. I listen to their tones and inflections. Have we been attacked again? Has Bush reintroduced the draft? Has someone been assassinated?

On the winding road to La Grasse, just as we pass out of Limoux into the lilting countryside, two triangular French fighter planes slice low through the blue sky, terrible and swift—schoom-schoom—just like that, they disappear behind a hill. We cannot speak for miles.

But then we have to slow the car for a small brown dog struggling down the middle of the road ahead of us, lugging half a fat baguette in its mouth as it heads for a hiding place. He must have snatched it from someone's table as they prepared for lunch, and he is not going to give way to us as he waddles with his treasure. We hold back so not to worry him, and it is good to laugh again.

We walk up the hill to the old château in nearby Chalabre, which has recently been prepared for tourism after centuries as a private residence. The guides are dressed in medieval finery. The ancient edifice is spectacular, but not yet quite presentable after years of neglect. The old stables are open and there are horses draped with bright banners. Local high school students, dressed in medieval costumes, practice sham battles with pikes, wooden swords, shields, and helmets, like Celts and Normans, pretending to beat on each other for the tourists.

It is Easter in Languedoc. We are attending a jazz festival, "Swing a Mirepoix." There are French groups with names like Big Band Roquette and Pompon Swing and Hericot Rouge. It is entrancing to hear these intense, European musicians cooking hard on Ellington and Basie arrangements, and the beautiful chanteuses singing "Misty," "Here's That Rainy Day," and "Sophisticated Lady" in their bewitching French-intoned English. A peppy group of young men and women vocalize Charlie Parker and Lester Young riffs, making us realize more than ever that jazz is America's singular, artistic gift to the world. The French especially seem to cherish it.

A Spanish band called Batucada comes on: seventeen musicians and one petite chanteuse, all wearing light band jackets and jaunty Panama hats, performing rich, Latin swing under a covered dance floor in the open air market. The music throbs exotically around the ancient, medieval square. The crowd holds back, standing on the fringes of the dance floor, uncertain and shy in the face of such voluptuousness.

A small, squat woman appears in front of the bandstand, a black and gray lump in a worn coat, heavy shoes and support stockings, a fuzzy stocking cap pulled down over her sparse, ashen hair. She wears thick glasses and her lips are heavy and moist. Something is not quite right about her, something taken from her years ago, perhaps when she was born. She sways in front of the band, rolling her shoulders and waving her arms. She turns to face us, her lips forming the words that the glamorous chanteuse is singing.

She begins to move her feet, dipping and turning, her arms reach out as she circles heavily. She is joined on the dance floor by another kind of woman, perhaps even older, her face wrinkled, but her hair dyed a phosphorescent wine color, wearing a bright blue dress and high-spiked shoes that match the color of her hair. She is more mobile than the squat woman; her movement is stiff, but with an echo of fluidity. The two women dance, off by themselves, both lost in private memories and rapture.

They are joined by other solitary dancers, people drifting onto the floor, giving way to the irresistible rhythm. A few of them reach out to touch each other as they dance, but these are solitary acts. Then couples begin to come into the dancing, elderly and rigid in their steps, holding each other, turning and swaying slowly. I touch Suzanne on the shoulder. She looks at me, and then we make our way toward the floor through the standing crowd.

A very tall Spanish man comes onto the floor. He is older than the rest of us, a man in his eighties, straight as a soldier. He goes to the small, squat woman and embraces her, taking hold of her as a man might grasp the last precious remnant of his life, as if she is all that he has left. He subdues her wriggling movements, makes her step carefully, syncopated and erect, and their movement to the rhythm becomes subtle and proud.

As they dance he looks off, as if remembering things from years ago, when he was young and indestructible, things lost in fire and rubble and never won back, yet glimpsed distantly in this music, on a bright day on a dance floor, in a country not his own.